The Glass Christmas Ornament: Old & New

The Glass Christmas Ornament: Old & New

A Collector's Compendium And Price Guide

By Maggie Rogers with Judith Hawkins

TIMBER PRESS   P.O. BOX 92   FOREST GROVE, OREGON 97116

Photographs by Edward Gowans
Design by Clyde Van Cleve

THE GLASS CHRISTMAS ORNAMENT: OLD AND NEW
A COLLECTOR'S COMPENDIUM AND PRICE GUIDE
ISBN 0-917304-07-1
© Copyright 1977 by Timber Press   P.O. Box 92
    Forest Grove, Oregon 97116
Library of Congress Cataloging in Publication Data
Library of Congress Catalog Card Number: 77-16741
PRINTED IN THE UNITED STATES OF AMERICA

Dedicated to
Harry Wilson Shuart
and
Our Families

For advice and generous assistance we thank

Mr. Harry Wilson Shuart, Suffern, New York
Mrs. John F. Hook, Portland, Oregon
Mrs. John T. Crowley, Omaha, Nebraska
Mr. Phillip V. Snyder, New York City, New York
The Corning Glass Museum, Corning, New York
Ruth E. Erisman, Lancaster, Pennsylvania
Mr. Harvey W. Steele, Portland, Oregon
The Staff, Multnomah County Library, Portland, Oregon
Mr. Robert Kramer, Portland, Oregon
Mr. Allen Simmons, Portland, Oregon
Mrs. Betty Jo Hubbard, Portland, Oregon

We gratefully acknowledge ornaments photographed from the collections of

Mrs. Joy Abele
Mrs. Larcel Abendroth
Mrs. Marianne Anderson
Mr. William Bingham
Mrs. Joseph E. Bonner
Mr. Gordon Branstator
Mr. Ed Cauduro
Master Simon Cheesman
Mrs. John T. Crowley
Mrs. Sandy DuBose
Mrs. Madlyn Fosmark
Mrs. Theodore R. Gamble, jr.
Mrs. Marjorie Geddes
Mr. and Mrs. Donald W. Green III
Mrs. Evelyn L. and Gloria Greenstreet

Miss Mary Hamblet
Mrs. Genevieve Hamill
Mrs. Kittredge Hawkins
Mrs. J. Stacy Hendrix
Mrs. Marion Hilton
Mr. Wallace K. Huntington
Dr. and Mrs. Lynn S. Husband
Mrs. Pat Krogman
Mr. Eric Ladd
Mr. and Mrs. William C. Lawrence
Mr. Christopher E. Leonard
Mr. and Mrs. Michael Madden
Mrs. Vicki Miles
Misses Elizabeth and Barbara Mott and Mr. Dewitt Mott
Mrs. Thomas J. Niedermeyer
Mrs. John Piper
Mr. Don Price
Mr. William C. Ralston
Mrs. Elizabeth Ann Ray
Mrs. Wayne R. Rogers
Dr. and Mrs. Lawrence Serrurier
Mr. Phillip V. Snyder
Mrs. Margaret Soumie
Mrs. Susan Stetson
Miss Alice Swanman
Miss Marjorie Wooton

Contents

Preface

This book began as a lark. One Christmas, looking at the ornaments we had collected here and there over many years, Judy and I decided that it would be fun, and easy—just like "water off a duck's back"—to do a book about them. My collection had begun the first year of my marriage, when I made ornaments from all kinds of fancy pasta on papier mache balls because my husband's salary as a resident physician hardly allowed for such frivolities. Judy's collection, started by her mother, had grown until her tree-trimming ritual took three full days during which the children had to be taken out of the house by her husband. Since we had so many and such a variety of ornaments, a pretty little picture book about them seemed a simple enough undertaking.

Two years later, our conception of the book has changed. We discovered only two books and a few articles about old ornaments in general, and glass ones, in particular. Instead of a "fluffy" picture book, we have tried to make a detailed, helpful, easy-to-use aid for anyone who loves glass Christmas ornaments and wants to know more about them. We have tried to answer the questions of what, how, when, where, and why: the origin of the Christmas tree and of the custom of decorating it; some of the myths and legends surrounding certain ornaments; the various methods of manufacturing glass ornaments from the beginning to the present time; the geographical areas and periods from which ornaments have come; the ways to identify ornaments and to judge their rarity; the range of kinds of ornaments in terms of subject matter and form; the newer 'Collectors' Series'; some of the major

Christmas tree, resplendent with 3,000 glass ornaments, decorated by Judith Hawkins each holiday season.

importers and the rate of importation in various years; how to repair broken ornaments.

The two years during which we worked on the book have changed our lives significantly. We began studying German in earnest, paid countless visits to the library, and were impelled to visit the Christmas ornament world in Bavaria. We have learned much about the fascinating process of putting a book together, the vexing problems of photographing objects which reflect a great deal of light, the responsibility of handling other people's fragile treasures. Parts of the task proved anything but simple: the pulling together of information about a subject on which much of the available information had to come from personal contacts with other collectors; the struggle to make something coherent and useful out of multitudinous, and at first glance unrelated, bits and pieces.

Yet we've been so lucky. Our search for information has resulted in new and devoted friendships. For encouragement in the beginning we are especially indebted to Jean Crowley of Omaha, Nebraska, who urged us to continue despite initial obstacles. Margaret Soumie of Portland, Oregon was a steady source of support. And just at the point where we were at a loss for highly specific details, Harry Wilson Shuart of Suffern, New York, from his extensive knowledge, bailed us out with unbelievable skill and generosity of spirit. Especial thanks is due the staff of the Multnomah County Library of Portland, all of whom were not only unfailingly helpful but gracious in providing that help. With steady assistance from our publisher, designer, photographer, and others, we've solved many of the problems we've encountered. Of course, we haven't found all the answers, and we own any errors or omissions which remain.

No one can ever really estimate the toll that writing a book takes on others. Our husbands, children, and friends endured, and we thank them. But in the end they, too, found themselves ensnarled, captured, and fascinated. Really, who couldn't be? Christmas ornaments are so beautiful!

Maggie Rogers
June 1, 1977
Portland, Oregon

Foreword

Collectors today understand the importance of ephemera, minor decorative arts, and the seemingly unimportant items of yesterday. Toys have been seriously collected for many years but related fields often neglected. The Christmas tree ornament was relegated to the garage sale and eccentric collector until the 1970s.

Any new field of collecting takes on added importance with the publication of historical materials. Articles and books have appeared during the 1970s to help the collector, indeed to encourage the beginner to join in the search. This is the first book about the Christmas ornament that is written with the needs of the collector in view.

To be of use, the book needs several parts. The basic history of Christmas holiday and Christmas customs are, of course, included here for general background and frame of reference. Manufacturers and their importance are recorded. Identification charts explaining the manufacturing techniques, the scarcity, the country of origin, the significance of the design, and other useful information are included. Collectors will appreciate the organized tables that make it easier to identify an ornament quickly. We particularly like the short chart giving the chronology of caps, hangers, and marking regulations—a quick dating guide for collectors.

The many black and white and color photographs show the humorous, the rare, and the beautiful ornaments. Even if you only own a few Christmas ornaments you can enjoy the others shown in the book.

A book on Christmas tree ornaments would not be complete without a section on the new collectors series, started within the past few years. And, of course, the hints on repairs will be of assistance. Best of all, the book is completely indexed—the aid needed by every researcher.

Collecting antiques has meant many things to us through the years. Among others it has been a chance to meet the interesting, famous, and diligent in the collector's world, and to have the opportunity to review books devoted to new fields of collectibles. This book is well-researched, well-written, and a needed addition to the Literature.

Ralph and Terry Kovel
June, 1977

*Deutsch Christbaum (German
Christmas tree) in Berlin, 1930.*

The Glass Christmas Ornament: Old and New

"Collecting" which was a phenomenon in the nineteen sixties in the United States became a mania in the seventies. Following the Vietnam War, America underwent a period of rapid and disorienting change, and many people, especially young people, longed for the security and sentiment of the past. For the first time, relatively inexpensive items without great age were eagerly pursued at the same time that fine antiques were commanding a good market. This awakening to our American heritage led thousands, having enough money and ample leisure time, on the search for old, interesting and nostalgic things. These Americans became deeply involved with their collections, studying and enjoying them not only for their own intrinsic worth, but as investments for the future as well. While there have always been many long-time collectors of Christmas memorabilia, there are now growing numbers of discriminating individuals who have come to appreciate those unique symbols of the Christmas season—tree ornaments—both old and new. Recognizing in them a sense of continuity, they discover they can relate Christmas and all its trappings to its connotation of family closeness, holiday festivities, and deep religious meaning. And they find it well within their means to collect ornaments. Better still, the variety from which to choose is infinite: glass, wood, wax, metal, paper, lint, celluloid, papier mache, spun glass, yarn, natural objects, plastic, or fabric.

Detail of old German Christmas Tree, Berlin, 1930.

Some ornament collectors like new ornaments or ornaments of a particular type, but the majority seem to prefer the beautiful blown-glass creations of old Europe which added so much to the lives of their parents and grandparents before them. Nothing can match the fantasy of a Christmas tree glowing with old glass globes and whimsical glass figures, reflecting the brilliance of the Christmas tree lights.

Just why do we decorate Christmas trees? And where and when did Christmas really begin? It was a long time ago. A brief look at winter traditions and legends will not only help form a background to understand the significance of ornaments, but also deepen the association the ornament collector can make with his collection and its historic meaning.

The Origin of Christmas, Santa Claus, and the Tree

1

While winter brings its own peculiar stark beauty, man from the earliest ages has sought to relieve the tedium and drabness of a long winter with color and gaiety. The early Romans celebrated Saturnalia, beginning on December 17th and continuing for seven days, to mark the end of the earth's retreat from the sun and to extol its re-birth as each successive day grew longer. It was a wild holiday, honoring Saturnus, first king of Latium who was the god of seed-grains and sowing. Preceded by animal sacrifices, the bacchanalia was a period of uninhibited feasting and gambling. Trees were worshipped for their magical qualities and evergreens, symbols of eternal life, were studded with flowers and used everywhere as decorations. Candles were lighted freely to help strengthen the weak but reviving sun. Wax tapers and little terra cotta dolls were exchanged as gifts. The chosen King of Saturnalia presided over the week's revelries, and at the end of his week's reign he was sacrificed to insure the productivity of the soil.

Another pagan festival, the Kalends, was celebrated in the Teutonic and Celtic areas of northern and western Europe, commencing in early November. By the 10th century the *Dies Natalis Invicti Solis* was celebrated in England as the pagan birthday of the unconquerable sun. Falling on December 25th between Saturnalia (December 17th) and the Kalends of January, this holiday coincided with the majority of mid-winter festivals of Europe and Asia where it was the chief fete day of the Phrygian god, Attis, in Asia Minor, and of Mithras in Persia.

Early Greeks as well as Romans revered trees; their fir trees were sacred not only to Neptune, but to Cybele, mother of the gods and wife of Saturn, who was responsible for the fecundity of fields and flocks and the personification of energy animating the earth. The Greeks dedicated their pine trees to Bacchus, god of vegetation, while the Romans consecrated them to two gods—Pan, deity of forests and hunters, and Neptune, god of springs and streams.

During the early centuries of the Christian era, these declining pagan beliefs and practices existed together with increasingly significant Christian observances. But it was not until the 4th century A.D. that there was a concensus as to when the birth of Christ should be celebrated. In the year 350 A.D., Pope Julius, acting upon the advice of his religious advisors, designated December 25th the Holy Day. Early Christians kept the day as one of fasting and gloom. As the great Roman empire crumbled and missionaries spread

Christianity throughout central and western Europe, Pope Gregory the Great, in 597, rather than outlawing paganism outright, wisely advised that pagan customs be assimilated into the church "for the greater glory of God." As a result, many pagan customs, though transfigured, remain today as cherished parts of our modern Christmas: the green tree, decorations of greenery, fire rites, gift exchanges, and the splendor of the Christmas table.

One early legend tells of the "first" Christmas tree. St. Boniface, the Apostle of Germany, was travelling through northern Germany. One day he happened upon a group of pagans at an oak tree near Geismar. They were preparing to sacrifice small Prince Asulf to the pagan god, Odin. The Saint convinced them to fell the blood oak instead. As it collapsed, a fir sapling sprang up in its place. Henceforward the conifer was revered as the tree of life, representing the true Christ and eternal life.

Another Christian legend relates to St. Nicholas, Bishop of Myra in Asia Minor, who, living in the 4th century, became important as the early representation of Father Christmas. As the patron saint of children, merchants, sailors, and bankers, he stands as a symbol of generosity to the poor. He once gave, according to the story, three bags of gold as dowries for three daughters of a poor man. The bags, stylized as three gold balls, later became sybolic of the gold balls used on Christmas trees, as well as the traditional sign of the pawn-broker. The legends of this saint, combined with the Teutonic legends of Thor and the later tales of Kriss Kringle, contribute to the figure of Santa Claus.

In northern Europe of the seventh century, Christian missionaries found pagans worshipping Thor, god of war. Thor was represented as an old man with a long beard. An awesome character, he roared through the heavens with crashes of thunder while he threw red firebolts of lightning. He lived among peoples of the North, fighting the gods of ice and snow, easing the dreaded threat of winter. Thor eventually evolved into the Father Christmas of Germany, first appearing as a two-sided personality, coming not only to reward, but to punish. The idea of joyous gift-giving found in the pagan celebration was maintained in the legend of the genial and generous old Bishop of Myra, while the concept of Santa Claus as the judge of good and bad children at Christmas seems to derive from Thor and his Teutonic background.

The location of the Claus residence at the North Pole with its snow and ice stems from the Germanic legends, but the origin of red as the traditional Christmas color remains a moot point. Did it derive from St. Nicholas' vibrant robes or Thor's brilliant firebolts?

During the Middle Ages liturgical dramas became an extremely popular form of moral instruction, learning, and entertainment for an illiterate populace. These Miracle or Mystery Plays portrayed the stories of the Bible but dealt most commonly with his Saints. One of the best-loved was the Paradise Play which told of the Creation and the Fall of Adam and Eve, usually performed during Advent leading directly into the celebration of Christ's birth. A fir tree hung with apples represented the Garden of Eden; it symbolized both the Tree of Life and the Tree of Knowledge of Good and Evil, and glass ball ornaments are said to stem from the apples on the Paradise Tree.

Miracle Plays were largely abandoned in the fifteenth century due to abuses and irreverence, but many people continued to decorate Paradise trees at Christmas to honor Christ's advent. In addition to the usual fruits, white wafers used in Communion, representing the saving fruit of the Eucharist, were hung on the branches. Subsequently, these wafers were replaced by cookies in various shapes—angels, stars, flowers, bells, and hearts. Later cookies made in the shapes of men and animals were added.

A lovely sixteenth century myth tells of an early Christmas tree, the first one decorated with candles. (No proof has ever been found that Luther had any tangible connection with the *Christbaum*.) It is said that Martin Luther, walking alone on a cold, dark night, gazed up at the sky filled with blazing stars. Deeply moved by its beauty, he went home and placed lighted candles on a tree to duplicate the brilliant stars of the winter sky.

The first recorded account of a decorated Christmas tree is found in a Strasbourg, Germany, manuscript, dated 1605, which reads: "They sat up fir trees in the parlors . . . and hung upon them roses cut from many colored paper, apples, wafers, gilt-sugar, sweets . . .". About this time the practice of erecting and decorating pyramids of wood began in Germany. Greens were twisted in garlands around the wood supports, and trimmed with tinsel and small glass balls. A candle placed on top was lighted to proclaim Christ the Light of the World. The first pyramid or *lichstock* to appear in the New World was decorated on Christmas Day, 1747, by the children of the Moravian Church in Bethlehem, Pennsylvania. These pyramids continued

A "Paradise Tree" – over the centuries glass ball were substituted for the apples.

4

to be used until the early 20th century.

When, in the mid-17th century, the Puritans came to power in England, Christmas celebrations in that country reverted to the more sober practices of an earlier day. Likewise the early Puritan settlers in New England shunned holiday revelry in favor of the more austere religious observances of their English faith. The settlers in the American South however, continued to enjoy Christmas in the traditional elegant fashion.

Word-of-mouth has it that the first Christmas tree in North America was set up by homesick Hessian soldiers at Trenton, New Jersey in 1776. The first appearance of Christmas trees in American homes is uncertain as well, but several early 19th century accounts demonstrate a growing use of the symbol. A sketch in John Lewis Krimmel's drawing book of Philadelphia, dated 1819-20, shows him at a table on which rests a decorated tree. A year later a diary account by Matthew Zahm of Bethlehem, Pennsylvania, mentions an expedition setting out to cut Christmas trees. Another early tree was decorated by Charles Follen, a German professor at Harvard in 1832, who mistakenly has been given credit for the first decorated tree in America. Still another is that of a minister, Pastor Henry Schwan of the Zion Lutheran Church, Cleveland, Ohio, who erected the first decorated tree to appear in a church. His congregation vigorously opposed its presence, considering it a pagan practice. The custom, however, became sufficiently widespread that Franklin Pierce set up a tree in the White House in the 1850s. His practice was continued by President Benjamin Harrison. President Theodore Roosevelt liked the idea, too, but concerned about excessive tree-cutting, was inclined to break the new tradition. Gifford Pinchot convinced him of the value of thinning and re-planting the forests. Thus, under Teddy Roosevelt a new forest industry was incidentally born.

It required a passage in time to complete the formation of Santa Claus' character which had its roots in the 4th century. One important element was Kris Kringle, who stems from the late 18th century. The Germans and the Swiss-born Germans settled in Pennsylvania held the belief that the Christ Child brought gifts to children on Christmas Eve, entering through the keyhole. He, the *Christkindel*, rode a gray or white mule, and treats were left out for both the rider and his steed. As English settlers arrived, *Christkindlein* or *Christkindchen* was corrupted into Kriss Krindle, and

This engraving was the first of Thomas Nast's Santas which was used as an illustration in Clement Moore's famous book, "A Visit from St. Nicholas," in 1864.

The Development of Tree Ornaments

following the publication of two books, *Kriss Krindle's Book,* in 1842 and *Kriss Krindle's Tree* in 1845, the language corruption became permanent.

As late as the nineteenth century, Santa Claus was said to travel on foot, on horseback, or even in a wagon. A famous poem written in 1822 abruptly changed this concept. Clement C. Moore wrote in "A Visit from St. Nicholas," better known as "The Night Before Christmas," of Santa's sleigh and reindeer and his yearly trip down the chimney.

To complete the portrait of the modern Santa Claus, Thomas Nast, the famous American cartoonist, did a series of drawings for *Harper's Weekly* from 1863 until 1886. The cartoons were heart-warming, portraying Santa Claus' yearly activities. As the series progressed, Santa became more and more corpulent and roseate, grew a copious beard, and became irresistible to millions. He remains as such today, a wonderful creature without whom the Christmas tradition would be the poorer.

The ornaments first used in the United States were simple and homemade. However reflecting the human desire for beauty they soon became more elaborate and appealing. An 1869 issue of *Harper's Bazaar* reveals this listing: "the snow-clad veteran, Santa Claus, his bag emptied of its treasures with which he has adorned the tree: globes, fruits, and flowers of colored glass, bright tin reflectors, and innumerable grotesque figures suspended by a rubber string. There were clowns with cap and bells, funny little men concealing their faces behind funnier masks, as they spring up and down; Bismarck leaping up Napoleon's shoulders, exaggerated seraphim with flapping wings, and strange-looking old women with heads larger than their bodies." This account is the first journalistic description of the glass-blown ornaments made by natives of the Thuringian mountains of Germany which were being brought by the tidal wave of German immigrants arriving daily in America.

Germany has contributed more immigrants to the United States than any other European country, with 6.95 million arriving between 1820 and 1974. Prudent, hard-working, and most of all, thrifty, they brought much of their heritage with them, including Christmas decorations.

The first glass ornaments on record to reach America came in 1865, brought by immigrating Palatinate families to the Pennsylvania Dutch area. By 1870, agents working with sources in Germany were importing them directly to the notable German settlements—New York (Yorktown Heights), Milwaukee, Philadelphia, and Brooklyn.

In this early period a few ornaments were blown by an American glass-maker, William A. DeMuth, who made silvered balls and chains of bead ornaments. He was listed in the New York Business Directory of 1854, and a division of his firm, the Brockway Glass Company, continues today. This factory was the first of many to be set up in New York and New Jersey by immigrant glass blowers.

These same immigrant glass-workers in New York and southern New Jersey were the creators of the heavy, kugel-like grapes and pears which, for many collectors today, represent the choicest items on their trees. They were originally blown to serve as replacement ornaments for broken ones, and were purchased primarily by residents in the Pennsylvania Dutch area. The earliest glass grapes featured a prominent central vein on the ornament which curled and twisted about, eventually forming the hanger from which to suspend the ornament. These were made around 1830-40 for use as decorative pieces. By the 1880s, both pear and grape ornaments were finished with an embossed cap which supported a brass ring for hanging. For years, it has been thought that these ornaments were European-made, but recent information from the Pennsylvania Historical Society confirms their American origin.

The first imported glass ornaments were sold on street corners; later they were distributed for sale in the toy shops and variety stores. In 1883, the Erlich Brothers of New York offered German-blown fancy glass balls in their Christmas catalogue. During the 1880s-90s, newspaper ads offered glass ornaments for sale during the holidays at both O'Neil's on Sixth Avenue and Bernard Myers on Chamber Street in New York City. A decade later, three pages of Christmas decorations appeared in a toy and doll catalogue published by Amos M. Lyon, a New York wholesaler.

The center of the German ornament world was the little village of Lauscha, sixty miles due north of Nürnberg. It early became a center of glass-making. In 1597, Protestant glass-makers, fleeing religious persecution in the German province of Swabia, established themselves in Lauscha where they could utilize the natural resources of wood, limestone, and sand to produce household glassware. Under a grant from the Duke of Coburg, they built the first "glass house." As

The fairy-tale village of Lauscha. Photo Courtesy of Philip Snyder.

the trade succeeded they began to produce glass toys, pharmaceutical items, bulls-eye glass for windows, as well as the usual utilitarian glassware.

One of these early glass-makers, Hans Greiner, developed a process for making hollow glass beads by forming small spheres from thin sections of glass tubing and silvering the insides. The bead industry grew and thrived. Indeed, the Lauschans discovered making the new holiday glass beads consumed fewer raw materials than solid beads, and they began blowing tubing into metal cylinders to form the beads. However, despite reduced material requirements, the Thuringian forests, from which they derived charcoal, were being seriously depleted by the growing demand for glass products. Therefore, they turned to cheap vegetable oil (such as turnip oil) or even paraffin to fuel a small lamp and so work the thin-walled tubes. Technological advances, including a small under-arm bellows which eased the job of forming the glass tubing, and a forge designed by George Greiner in 1820 (and later improved upon by Ludwig Müller), further simplified the process of bead-making. Soon Lauschans were shipping beads throughout Europe to milliners and jewelers in great numbers. Unfortunately their commercial bonanza was to prove short-lived.

In 1845 a glass factory was set up in Jablonec nad Nisou, a town in the Sudetanland of Czechoslovakia. There the creative Bohemians developed glass beads whose beauty far surpassed those of the Lauschans. Called the "pearls of Paris," they were made of molded porcelain, etched, and finished with a brilliant lustre of gold or silver, a process invented by a Dr. I. Weisskopf.

In desperation the Lauschans returned to making scientific instruments, glass eyes for the growing toy industry, and small glass toys. For amusement they blew thick-walled balls called "kugels," which they finished inside either with lead or zinc to achieve a shimmery effect. They then discovered they could produce a striated effect by swirling the lead solution inside the kugel, and finish it by adding colored wax to enhance the lustre of the ball. These balls were called either "schecken" (spotted, dappled) or "plumbum" (lead). Both early kugels and schecken were corked, not capped; a loop fitted through the cork for hanging. In the meantime, the Lauschans experimented with the Bohemian silvering method, hoping to discover their secret. A glass-maker, Dr. Louis Greiner-Schlotfeger, finally succeeded and used it to silver the heavy kugels. The finish on the kugels was mirror-like, but their great weight permitted their use only as ceiling decorations. They hung suspended from wooden crowns which attached to the ceiling, catching the light as they moved.

A gas works was built in Lauscha in 1867. This new facility gave glass-blowers for the first time a readily regulated flame enabling them, in turn, to produce thin-walled glass products with great ease and facility. The integration of these various techniques and processes set the stage for the Christmas tree ornament industry—called by many "Germany's last great folk art." Lauschan glass-blowers, following the Greiner-Schlotfeger model and using a glass flame on thin-walled tubing, were soon creating many shapes in delicate glass—balls, cones, fruits—and Lauscha's future was assured. No one could ever have guessed how well! Many collectors think the first figural ornaments were pine cones blown into baking molds while others say the first hollow glass tree decorations, other than balls, were icicles blown from a solid piece of glass.

The demand for ornaments increased so rapidly that Greiner-Schlotfeger, and other Lauschan glass-blowers appealed for help in both Steinach and Steinheid. Lauscha and Steinheid became the twin-villages of ornament production. Indeed, in 1888-89, an article appeared in a Sonneberger commercial journal which reported that the Christmas ornament business had surpassed the toy industry in sales volume. This is significant since Sonneberg was the world's toy mecca. Ornaments, like toys, were mass-produced in the peasants' homes and at the turn of the century it was estimated that 75% of the population of the Thüringian region was engaged in "cottage industries."

Blowing and painting glass ornaments in a Sonneberg "werkstatt," 1902.

Ornaments were sold by the "publisher" system, the publisher being the middleman between the manufacturer and the retailer. He peddled from the house or by mail order, providing sample displays. A buyer might commission a single publisher to select the best available stock for him. Alternately a buyer might travel to Lauscha and Steinheid to compare merchandise from publisher to publisher. Most orders were ready to ship by May 1st. In turn the publisher gave the orders to the cottage glass-blowers, who were fairly independent in both their designs and how they spent their time. However the publisher determined the prices of the ornaments. The craftsman received a pitifully small reward for his efforts. A family of six, working an eleven-hour day, reportedly received about three dollars a week.

The Manufacture of the
German Ornament

Christmas tree ornaments were made in the homes of German glass-blowers and involved the labor of an entire family, in a process that remained essentially unchanged until World War II. Having perfected the simple ball ornaments, they tried their hands at more difficult shapes, relying increasingly on the skill and artistry of the mold-makers. It is estimated that over 5,000 different molds were made between the 1870s and 1940. The mold-maker first sculpted his figure in clay or wood, greased it with fat, and then cast it, one-half at a time, in plaster-of-Paris. These two halves were glued to iron tongs to complete the mold. Plaster-of-Paris is ideally suited to this purpose as it readily adapts to alternate heating and cooling without shrinking or distorting the glass shell in it.

By the 1920s and thirties, most of the old molds (formsachen) were owned by one Herr Wittmann of Lauscha who had a small ceramic factory and supplied the entire industry of glass-blowers. Known as the "mother molds," most of them disappeared upon the death of Wittmann. The whereabouts of the majority of the molds is uncertain, according to the late eminent toy expert of the Sonneberg Toy Museum, Frau Emmy Lehmann.

The period between 1890 and 1920 was known as the "fantasy period," the time when the most creative ornaments were produced. Free to make whatever suited their own fancies, the glass artisans blew "whimsies" in addition to their usual "bread and butter" ornaments which formed the basis of their livelihood. Many of these ornaments were "free-blown" but some required the special talents of the mold-makers. One such ornament was a glass Eiffel, another is the baby-in-the-bath-tub ornament. Still another is the rabbit emerging from the egg ornament.

Since the glass-maker relied so heavily on the molds for the majority of the ornaments produced, individual families strove to achieve distinction by the colors and patterns they applied to the ornaments. Using a wide range of mold-blown geometric shapes and figurals, the Greiner family as an example preferred a pastel combination while the Müller group chose a configuration of gold, red, blue, and white. Pastel colors, in general, were more popular in the early days as they resembled the coloration of early 19th century Christmas tree decorations (confekt) of sugar and pale-tinted frostings.

In the workshop (werkstatt) attached to every home

Old mold showing the Santa Claus ornament which was mouth-blown into it.

where ornaments were made, the father and his sons worked at an ordinary table. It was fitted with pedal bellows used to regulate the gas burner and foot-operated molds for each worker. Working over the hot flame with small glass blobs, previously prepared, the blower would place the molten bubble into the bottom of the mold quickly, close it, and continue blowing until the thin glass wall fully conformed to the shape of the mold. Opening it, he removed the clear glass shape which would be finished by the other members of the family. Birds, Santas, cones, nuts, fruits, baskets, and houses were mold-blown. Ornaments formed "free-hand" (without mold assistance) included trumpets, lyres, anchors, hearts and crosses, butterflies with spun glass wings, and vases with graceful handles.

In another corner of the crowded room sat the women, finishing the ornaments. One would fill each ornament one-quarter full of the silvering solution with a *"stackheber,"* resembling a turkey-baster. The silvering was a solution of silver nitrate, lactose (milk sugar), and lime. A young girl next to her, holding as many ornaments as she could in her outstretched hands, would then shake them gently in warm water to coat the inner surfaces evenly, as irregular silvering would render an ornament unsalable. She then dumped the remaining solution from the ornaments into a large beaker where it would be chemically separated and re-used. The ornaments were next dipped into an aniline dye bath and hung upside down on a bed of nails to dry in a warm place.

A Lauschan family working together trimming glass ornaments in their simple home, 1902.

After the ornaments had dried overnight, they were dipped into tubs of various colored lacquers. (It is the lacquer on old ornaments which has a tendency to peel if the ornament is roughly handled or allowed to become damp.)

All family members shared in the final painting and decorating of the ornaments. Sometimes the details were hastily done; sometimes they were exacting, depending on the skill and disposition of the craftsmen. (By the 1920s German ornaments were painted by mouth-operated air brushes.) On some ornaments they spread colorless gelatin adhesive and then sprinkled gold, silver, or glass dust, or tiny glass beads called "Venetian Dew." To achieve a shimmering effect of snow, the ornament was dunked into a solution of gelatin and starch. Fluoride designs were sometimes etched onto surfaces in delicate traceries.

During all these processes, the long glass projection, the "pike," which the blower formed while blow-

*Market day in Lauscha, 1902,
going to meet the train to
Sonneberg, central shipping
depot.*

*The craze for air-ships was a
Christmas inspiration for an
artist at the turn of the century,
who had Santa riding a zepplin
to deliver toys. Ornament-
makers followed suit.*

ing the ornament, remained attached to the ornament.
Occasionally it was retained to serve as the handle on
an umbrella, handbell, or baby rattle ornament. Usually, however, the oldest child in the family scored the
pike with a little, sharp knife, and cleanly snapped the
protruding end off. Then the littlest children capped
each ornament, and packed them into boxes of a
dozen each.

Working conditions for the family were miserable.
F. W. Woolworth wrote the following account of the
little village in 1890:

> "They (ornaments) are made by the very poorest
> class there is in Europe and we were obliged to go
> into their dirty hovels to see what we could use. It
> was the dirtiest and worst-smelling place I was
> ever in . . . and this was only a sample of hun-
> dreds of houses in Lauscha. Out of 4,000 popula-
> tion there, Mr. Hunt (his assistant) says 3,500 of
> them are under five years of age."

Market day was Saturday and traditionally the
women brought the ornament boxes and sacks in baskets by train to Sonneberg which served as the central
depot for both ornaments and toys. In bad weather it
was not unusual to see the women knee-deep in the
muddy country lanes. The baskets were carried on the
back and were at least one yard high and several feet in
diameter. Often another basket, three by five feet, was
piled on top.

Ornaments became more elaborate as time passed,
both in design and trim. Embellishments included the
use of silk thread, chenille, tinsel, wool thread, swags,
tassels, and crinkly wire. Some ornaments had fabric
flowers, leaves, and "tucksheer," a kind of flocking
which is green and was used to represent foliage. Stiff
spun glass appeared as angel, bird, and butterfly
wings. Tinsel which had first been used on French
military uniforms was used freely on fancy flower
baskets, hanging lamps and vases, air balloons, egg
zepplins, boats and swings. Often embossed pictures
of sentimental subjects (*glanzbilder-reliefs*), made originally to adorn Christmas cakes (*lebkerchen*), were
glued on, to make an ornament especially appealing.
Originally the glanzbilder were printed in black on a
pastel background, tinted, varnished, dusted with
metallic powder, cut, and finally embossed—all by
hand. A new printing process slowly emerged so that
by 1830, chromolithography made possible the production of "scraps" on a grand scale. Old glanzbilder
on ornaments can be distinguished from new because
the old scraps were printed on a heavy paper, var-

nished on one side only, and the backs are usually yellow from age.

One single person, F. W. Woolworth of five and dime fame, is largely responsible for the huge numbers of ornaments which appeared in the United States over the years. But even he initially failed to recognize their tremendous sales potential. Owner of only one small store in Lancaster, Pennsylvania at the time, he was coerced into purchasing twenty-five dollars worth of ornaments while on a buying trip to Meyer and Schoenaman in Philadelphia to select dolls. The wholesaler agreed to refund his money should they fail to sell. Woolworth's supply was exhausted in several days. The next year an even larger order proved insufficient to meet the demand. Convinced, Woolworth made his first buying trip abroad in 1890, and travelled to Lauscha to purchase ornaments and marbles first-hand for his growing network of stores in America.

A letter written on April 17, 1909, confirms the popularity of the glass ornament in America:

> "While in Sonneberg I gave a large order, over 1,500 gross (about 216,000) for Christmas tree ornaments and I am pointed out on every corner of the street as the big buyer of tree ornaments and they tackle me everywhere trying to sell me more . . ."

Store records note that Woolworth had sold at least 25 million dollars worth, all for nickels and dimes! Later Woolworth's importing business was taken over by George Franck, who had started an importing firm in Baltimore in 1868. (The Franck Company was to become one of the major ornament-importing firms in America before the second World War.) Woolworth led the way and soon tree ornaments became bestsellers at other dime stores, Kresge, Newberry's, etc., as well.

Woolworth made another contribution to the ornament industry when, in a suit filed against the United States government in 1909, he managed to have modified the classification of Christmas ornaments from toys to that of glass articles. This greatly reduced the tariffs levied on imported ornaments. Tariffs affect both the type and quality of imports the United States receives, and they played a vital role in the Christmas ornament business over the years. Lower duties have consistently been assessed on goods originating in Japan, Austria, West Germany, and Italy than on those from Poland, Russia, Czechoslovakia, and East

The Christmas Ornament Tycoon

F.W. Woolworth

Sixteen Unusually Beautiful Fancy Glass Orna
The Assortment We Recommend
Five-inch red, white and blue boat with gilt mast; two balloons, 6 inches and 4 inches in height; basket with har green imitation fern; 4-inch trumpet and 3½-inch saxopho: and parrot with glass tail mounted on spring snap; larg Claus face and tinkling bell; closed umbrella with glass five fancy oblongs and reflectors, hand decorated in beautif and with tinsel wire and cord. Shpg. wt., 1¾ lbs.
69K6630—Per box of **16**.........................$

Ornaments were commonly advertised in Christmas catalogues as well as being sold in stores. Sears featured Lauschan ornaments in their 1910 Christmas catalogue for approximately 6c each!

Germany under terms of the 'most favored nation' agreement, part of the Hawley-Smoot Act of 1930.

The Rise of Competition in the Christmas Ornament Trade

Backed by Wooworth's empire in the United States, Lauscha and Steinheid, Christmas ornament capitals of the world, had no real competition until 1940, even though its production was interrupted by World War I. German ornaments were still plentiful in 1914, but by 1915, supplies were running low as the result of the U.S. embargo on German imports.

A few American toymakers tried to fill the gap, producing some amateurish twisted-ball ornaments and irregular shapes. The Americans found they lacked the know-how of the German glass-blowers, and both the brittle American glass and the red dye which took on a brownish cast prevented making acceptable ornaments. Thus, in 1920, when the fine German goods reappeared, the Germans had no difficulty regaining their supremacy in the ornament trade.

Germans are migratory people, and they wandered freely for centuries throughout central Europe. Realizing the advantages of a cheaper labor market, German capital moved into Austria in the early twenties. One German glass-blower, Herr Josef Eggeling, settled in Vienna in 1914, establishing the Wiener Christbaumschmuck-Fabrik. The company first produced papier-mache tree decorations, but following World War I, branched out, making beautiful glass creations. It was the first company of its kind, and the largest in Austria, managing to survive the second World War. Most glass-blowing was done as a "cottage industry" by transplanted Germans in the old German tradition, and Austrian ornaments are often difficult to distinguish from German.

Czechoslovakian artisan decorating a "point" at the time-honored firm of Jablonex nad Nisou.

Another of Germany's neighbors, Czechoslovakia, had a "cottage glass industry," and Czech artisans operated from their homes in Vsetin in Moravia until 1925, and thereafter in Bohemia, long famed for its exquisite glass. Work centered around Kraluv Dvur and Horice and in Bratislava. The first Czechoslovakian glass house had been established in Globaumits in 1845. In those early days they made a variety of glass trinkets, stars, candelabra, vases, and little glass baskets. By 1905, the Czechs had found a ready market for silver beaded Christmas ornaments. These were made in many colors, assembled on wires in a variety of geometric shapes, the beads being interspersed with glass bars, rings, and larger balls when warranted. Many familiar objects were reproduced in bead forms as well as beaded tree tops in the shape of stars. Some bead ornaments were three dimensional. By the 1920s, the Czechs were also producing glass balls and figural ornaments of all kinds, many direct copies of the German ones. The glass Czech Santa Claus, in contrast to the one made in Lauscha-Steinheid, substitutes the Christmas tree for a bag of goodies. More Czechoslovakian beaded ornaments exist than glass forms, but both are still made today. The industry flourished under the aegis of the Jablonex Corporation in Jablonec nad Nisou even though the country has never received any real reprieve from the high duty imposed by the United States. While a major source of glass ornaments, Czechoslovakia never approached the output of the Germans.

Poland, according to Mr. Wysocki, a present-day executive at the ornament co-operative, Coopexim, in Warsaw, produced her first glass Christmas ornaments in 1930, although she did not export them until 1934-35. The Polish people were largely agricultural, but in the early thirties, the country turned its efforts toward industrialization. With a cheap labor market available, Poland made great quantities of balls; many typical, large pear-shaped forms with a tip on the bottom; and a few rare figurals—mainly hand-blown simple shapes with the body details painted on. There were no Santas or bells. However, Poland is known for the beauty of the reflector or "indents" she made in profusion, and which sold in America by the thousands.

Typical Polish "indent."

Indents were made by almost every country in the ornament field. But the Polish ones were more beautiful in spite of the fact that they were cruder and generally smaller in scale than most. The Polish indents were more frequently painted in floral motifs and were commonly frosted with snow and dusted with silver or gold glitter.

To make a reflector or indent, the gaffer would heat one side of the ornament form over a hot flame, and press a plaster mold in the side of the form to the desired depth. (Early Lauschan blowers used a piece of coal or a twig.) The inside of the ornament was silvered as usual but the outside of the concavity was painted in a spectrum of colors so that they reflect against one another—pure Christmas romance—especially if the ornament is Polish, the colors of which were brighter and more varied than those of any other country. The Polish glass-blowers made indents in many different geometric shapes, occasionally with multi-sided indentations. Some of Poland's crafts may

German "indents" from the Greiner factory in Lauscha, East German; another branch of the Greiner family operates the Elias Greiner Vettersohn Company in Lauscha, producing many ornaments as well.

15

be deemed inferior, but never her Christmas ornaments!

Japan, as well, failed to overtake Germany's lead in the glass ornament industry, although she took a creditable second place. Following World War I, Japan became the world's largest toy exporter. The country underwent a rapid and significant trade expansion, and a "snow drift" of both ornaments and tree lights poured into the United States beginning in 1925. The cry heard throughout Japan was "Produce better articles cheaper!" The ornaments they produced may have been cheaper, but they certainly weren't better. Early attempts were crude; the colors on the ornaments were harsh, the glass shattered easily. Few were figurals (Santas, birds, chicks, lanterns, etc.), most were either ball forms or geometric shapes. The Japanese creations have none of the delicate quality and fragile beauty of their European prototypes.

In the early days of the industry, ornaments were made in Japanese homes, but by the late twenties, small manufacturers set up factories with some mechanization. These ornaments were then finished by Japanese children, the father of the family supervising the work of his young children. Many of them were to die from lead poisoning and tuberculosis due to the high lead content of the silvering compound they used in treating the ornaments. (Many European children died also.) By the thirties, Japan was considered a "most favored nation" and had a definite duty advantage in her principal export market, the United States. With the number of European ornaments dwindling just before World War II, Japan stepped up her production and was responsible for 93% of all ornaments shipped into America. This trade was abruptly interrupted when war was declared between Japan and the United States in 1941.

It is intriguing to note that Christmas was not widely celebrated by the Japanese until they became familiar with the ornaments they were making. Treating Christmas like a secular holiday for children, they, too, decorated trees.

In the thirties two attempts were made by known American glass firms to enter the trade on a minor scale. Around 1935, a Newark, New Jersey glassblower, Angelo Paione, had begun to create ornaments while at the Premier Glass Works Inc. (No examples of his work remain.) He left Premier to establish his own firm, the Paragon Glass Company, which later re-located in Maine. Using molds and compressed air, the ornaments were distinctive in that both the silvering and lacquering were applied on the exterior of the ornament for added brilliance and durability. The silver solution that Paione used was of his own manufacture. The family-owned firm discontinued manufacture of Christmas ornaments in 1974, and is now making industrial glass.

The other American firm making ornaments in this period was the Paper Novelty Products Company which produced a simplistic set of glass ornaments depicting Snow White and the Seven Dwarfs, the first known American figurals of silvered glass. Made in Brooklyn, New York, with rights from Walt Disney and sold under the name, Doubl-Glo, the figures were not a market success due to lack of detail and general appeal. During these years other glass factories were making ornaments, but with so little success that their efforts have left no trace. The Americans were not to make any real contribution to the ornament field until the Corning Glass Company began to mass produce Christmas ornaments in the early forties.

With the onset of World War II, the supply of ornaments from Europe and Japan was halted. As an article in *Life* magazine commented, "... the war has reached its long tentacles in the coziest corners ... the world of Christmas!" Through the foresighted efforts of long-time American importer of Christmas ornaments, Max Eckardt, and his good friend, Bill Thompson, of Woolworth's 'Five and Dime,' America at last was to dominate the area so long held by the Europeans.

Max Eckardt has played a leading role in modern ornament history. A native of the Lauschan region, he spent his boyhood in close touch with both ornaments and toys. He emigrated to the United States when he found advancement too slow in Germany. A few years later he and his brother established an import firm, appropriately called Brothers Eckardt, trading in toys and glass ornaments. In 1920, the firm decided to concentrate on ornaments, under the new name, Eckardt und Sohn, and discontinued importing toys and dolls. Adopting still another name, "Shiny Brite," in 1935, they became the largest firm in America dealing with Christmas ornaments and decorations. (It was sold in 1965 to Eckmar Corporation and to Poloron Products in 1971.)

Max Eckardt, between 1937 and 1939, convinced Corning Glass Works in Corning, N.Y. that war in Europe was inevitable. He managed to persuade them that they could manufacture Christmas ornaments as

The Mass Produced Ornament Dominated the Trade

The Corning Glass ribbon machine which mass produces Christmas ornaments at speeds faster than a machine gun fires bullets. Photo courtesy, Corning Glass Museum.

well as light bulbs on their newly patented "ribbon" glass-blowing machine. The machine had been designed in 1926, and perfected in 1934. Mr. Thompson of Woolworth's, at the same time, also gambling that war was imminent, offered to place a huge order with Corning if the company would convert the machine to produce ornaments. By early December, 1939, Corning shipped 235,000 ornaments to Woolworth's for holiday sales, machine-blown and machine-lacquered. The next year Corning shipped its first order of clear glass blanks to Max Eckardt's new "Shiny Brite" plant in New Jersey for silvering and finishing, an arrangement still in force today. Corning also supplied blanks to George Franck and Delta and Colby Glass—all firms who did their own decorating (by silk screen stenciling, hand-painting or by semi-automatic machines) and distributing. The Franck firm was eventually purchased by the Marathon Company, and re-formed under the name of Marathon-Franck in 1974.

Using a mix of sand, soda ash, and lime, and a 2800° temperature, the Corning plant produced 400 ornaments a minute, two million a week, so uniform that they could, with standardized packaging, be shipped without fear of breakage. Molten glass was fed into the ribbon machine, and as it moved along a belt, jets of air blew bubbles which were forced into molds. Completely automatic, the ornaments were inspected for flaws by polariscope; silvering, lacquering, and the removal of pikes was performed by machines. They were then sorted, packed, and shipped. Offered in 180 different styles and sizes, Corning made bells, oblongs, pyramids, lanterns, diamonds, indents, pine cones, acorns . . . to name a few. The company made one glass Santa Claus for two years: 1939-40. *Business Week* in December, 1941, reported: ". . . estimates for cash outlays for Christmas ornaments this year run between 3-4 million dollars, retailing for 5¢ and 10¢ each."

The needs of war caused shortages of metals and other raw materials used in the American ornament trade, so Eckardt, under the name "Shiny Brite," was forced to decorate the clear Corning glass balls with a minimum of paint which was usually applied in stripes or similar simple patterns. Occasionally a lone piece of tinsel would extend through the center of the ornament, a feeble attempt to impart a little sparkle to the form.

At the close of the war, Max Eckardt was the world's largest ornament producer. Due to the fire hazard arising from the use of potentially explosive silver nitrate and lacquer, Shiny Brite in the late 40s and early 50s re-located in four smaller plants scattered through New Jersey. By 1976 operating costs had forced Shiny Brite to amalgamate into a single operation in Batesville, Mississippi.

The only imports Shiny Brite handles today are tree-top ornaments ("points"), which are difficult to make and have long been an old European specialty. (Domestically only Colby Glass makes "points.")

In the late 1960s, Corning, for the first time since the early days of the war, returned to decorating and selling ornaments under its own name, as well as supplying blank glass ornaments to Shiny Brite and others in the business.

Brief mention should be made of other firms manufacturing ornaments during the war, although not much is known about them: the Marks Glass Company, Boston; the K and W Glass-Works, Bergen, N.J.; and the U.S. Glass Manufacturers, Brooklyn, N.Y.

Post-war "points" from the Greiner Company, Lauscha, East Germany. Old "treetops", available in many sizes, can range in price from $3-$15. Newer "points" can be purchased from $2-$6, depending on quality, size, and condition.

Developments in the Ornament Trade Since World War II

Central Europe emerged from the war totally devastated. The Potsdam Agreement following the surrender of Germany in 1945 neatly split the Thuringian ornament-producing area in half. Lauscha-Steinheid and Sonneberg fell into the Eastern Democratic Republic, controlled by the Russians; Coburg, annexed to Bavaria in 1923, and Neustadt became a part of the Western Federal Republic, governed by the three Western allies. Communication between these glass centers was severed. Stringent living conditions forced many East Germans and some Sudetanese from Czechoslovakia to flee to West Germany. The West Germans, faced with overcrowding and runaway inflation, were struggling to overcome the ravages of war as well, and their recovery was slow. The old glass-makers finally managed to establish a new "glass-house" in Neustadt, despite the loss of needed raw materials which came from Sonneberg across the border. By 1950, they were underway. Even though about seven firms are operating in West Germany today—the best known being the Oberfrankische Glas un Spielzeug in Neustadt and the Suddeutsche Benda Christbaumschmuck in Barnsdorf—(the famous Lanissa Company recently shut down)—at a level of monetary success never seen before, the era of the independent imaginative craftsman has passed, and few truly unique ornaments will ever be made again. In 1977, it is estimated that only 50-60 families are engaged in hand-blowing ornaments, and that only

West German blower at now-defunct Lanissa Factory finishing details on a tea-pot.

Adding "frosting" to the finished ornaments at the once very-active Lanissa factory, a few years after the close of World War II.

8% of all ornaments being produced are handblown.

Today 80% of West German ornaments are for the American trade; the remaining orders are from Europe, many for use in Germany. As in "olden times," buyers travel to Neustadt where they may visit the show-room of the West German Ornament Manufacturers (Oberfrankische Glas) and place their orders. There they may choose from the many different silvered ornament selections or may opt for the new clear glass ornaments, shaped into figural patterns and lightly touched in gold to highlight certain features on the ornaments. The order is then "farmed out" to smaller firms which operate from their owners homes as they did years ago. Or the buyers may deal directly with the individual craftsmen, although this route may prove more time-consuming. Much of the magic still remains in these work-shops attached to the side of the comfortable houses where the ornaments are still being blown and decorated today. In two of these, the Fritz Seiler Company and the O. and M. Langhammer Company in Neustadt, accomplished blowers fashion beautiful and precise ornaments at the rate of 100-120 dozen a day, which are silvered, hand-decorated, and finished largely by immigrant workers. (Machines are producing ornaments at a rapid rate in the work-shops as well.) Few young Germans have entered the glass-blowing trade. In 1955, a school was set up to teach the art of ornament-blowing. Most of its graduates, however, are immediately enticed into factories making industrial and scientific glass where the pay is commensurate with their skill. Thus while Germany remains the largest of the ornament exporters, it seems unlikely that Germany will ever regain her dominance of the trade.

Today four East German companies continue to export ornaments, as well as Christmas bibelots and novelties. Those who stayed in the Eastern zone after the war found they had to operate through the Black Market, exchanging sacks of ornaments for vital items such as razor blades, coffee, and cigarettes. Many East German glass-makers refused to use either the "Made in East Germany" or "Made in Occupied Germany" labels on ornaments, preferring to smuggle their limited ornament production to West Germany for export under a West German tag. Now most ornaments are blown in Lauscha's government factory where quality of the goods has been slipping steadily. (Rising silver costs add to the problems.) They are still blown in what old molds have survived the war, and a few old-timers continue to make ornaments in their

The Werner Fischer family exhibiting some of their present-day stock in front of their glass-factory in Coburg, West Germany.

A contemporary home of an ornament-maker in Neustadt, West Germany; the workshop is attached to the side of the house.

A woman silvering ornaments by hand in a Neustadt, West German "werkstatt" in much the same way as in years past.

homes, using their own distinctive molds. (In contrast, new molds are now being made of porcelain, at a cost of about 1,000 Deutsche marks—$430!) In years to come, these ornaments being made by old East German blowers will be priceless as so few are still being made, and practically none leave the country. (Scarcely one-fourth of those made cross the border.)

A visitor to Neustadt today can look from a second story window and see both Sonneberg and Lauscha in the distance, hamlets nestled in the green Thuringian hills. Seemingly only a "stone's throw" away, formidable obstacles stand between East and West Germany. At the border is a complex barrier which deters even the strong-hearted. A strip of grass, heavily impregnated with land mines, lies behind the first fence at the edge of the Western zone. A tall wall of wooden posts demarks the next obstacle of guard dogs leashed onto long lines, but capable of moving about freely to patrol the grounds. Yet another high fence and mine field looms behind, In the background is a large out-post structure with soldiers keeping watch from the tower. Any person approaching the border is automatically photographed with a telephoto lens, and should any untoward activity occur at the first barrier, it will bring forth a large armored tank whose gun turret will fasten on the offender almost immediately.

The end of the road between West and East Germany. Straight ahead is the East German watch-tower, and just beyond, the villages of Lauscha and Steinheid and Sonneberg.

Life in East Germany is hard, and the pay scale of "cottage glass" is much lower than in West Germany. Being unable to leave, any young people attracted to ornament blowing are forced to work in the factory. Around 1972, as economic conditions improved, Demusa of Berlin, Kuhnert Egli Bachmann and Company, and Emil C. Wittag of Thuringia joined the government factory in producing fine ornaments for foreign gift shops, florist shops and better mail-order catalogues such as Neiman Marcus and the Horchow Collection in Dallas, Texas. Certainly the "most favored nation" clause in U.S. customs regulations has consistently affected divided Germany: East Germany is faced with higher tariffs than West Germany, and this is reflected in numbers of ornaments received in the United States. Of course, East Germany as a member of the Soviet 'bloc' has had her trade largely limited to the Comecan countries.

Czechoslovakia was the first country to return to Christmas ornament production following the war. Under a trade agreement between Czechoslovakia and the United States, the tariff rate of 55% as originally set in 1930, was reduced to 50% ad valorem in 1948 (for one year), and this proved an impetus to

Highly-skilled East German glass-blower fashioning ornamets at top speed over flames of gas burners.

21

Polish glass-blower and artist demonstrating their expertise at a trade fair. Trade fairs are held in centers annually throughout Europe to promote both commerce and good-will.

Booth at the Christmas Fair in Vienna, Austria, set up by the famous Austrian firm, Advent und Christbaumschmuck Decor, W. Zipser Company.

increased production. However over the years output first leveled off and then fell, as control of the country fell to the Communists and trade was largely oriented to the Soviet bloc. Two firms are operating today: Glass-export in Praha, and the old, established firm of Jablonex.

Poland, in 1947, started her comeback in the ornament world, and in spite of many economic and social problems, had become the world's third largest exporter of Christmas ornaments by the 1960s. The fact that Poland was the most devastated nation in Europe after the war makes her resurgence even more remarkable. In addition, she was not recognized as a "most favored nation" until 1970, and her exports to the U.S. were subject to high duties. Continuing to make ornaments similar to those made in the thirties and forties, Coopexim, a large collective in Warsaw, exports Polish ornaments today, primarily to the United States.

Austria, always a "most favored nation," has the distinction of making the most imaginative and detailed post-war ornaments. Austria recovered from the war with the help of American-aid funds, as did many Western European countries, and the glass-blowers struggled to re-build the machinery destroyed during the war. It has been reported that machines worth thousands of dollars were dismantled in order to obtain a single motor with which to operate their glass businesses. Glass-blowing was centered around Vienna. The old, prominent firm of Eggeling and Company was re-organized, and is today the major exporter of Austrian ornaments. Under new ownership of former plant manager Wolfgang Zipser, it has been moved forty miles north to the old Roman city of Traismauer. The firm is now known as Advent und Christbaum Decor. The business is smaller, but its ornaments are no less beautiful. They make a wide variety of ornaments using old motifs, but from new molds as most old molds were melted down to recover the metal during the war. In addition they have introduced many new designs, featuring distinctive painting as trim.

Japan, exporting heavily to the United States before the war, became the principal source of inexpensive ornaments (70% of the quantity) after the war. Beginning in 1947, she had both the advantage of a cheap labor market and a "most favored nation" status. By the 1960s, Japanese imports were thriving, but rising labor costs have reduced their competitive edge. Japanese ornaments during this period were largely small and miniature balls, frequently seen with a wire extending from the cap which was bound with colored or colored metallic paper.

Italy began much later, in 1955, exporting excitingly different glass figural ornaments—a seal balancing a ball on its nose, a harlequin, a Chinese girl holding a ping-pong racquet, and figures representing famous cartoon characters like Donald Duck and Mickey Mouse—and a few ball ornaments. The range of subjects is staggering, but they exhibit two serious flaws. The first results from the use of cheapening trims, such as feathers, cotton, pipe cleaners, maribou, and plush. The second is the tawdriness of some ornaments, such as the drunk mouse, the Krazy Kats, and a dreadful garish angel. In spite of occasional spottiness in the line, Italian figurals are choice.

Centered around the Lake Como region in Italy, the ornaments are blown in a number of small factories which form a loose association. Dario Moranduzzo is the largest producer of the three major firms in Italy. In the United States they are distributed by several companies, the best known being Silvestri, based in Chicago. Italian ornaments are so popular that they sell out virtually upon their arrival despite their comparatively high price tags. All these ornaments are handblown in the old manner, shaped by paddles as the glass bubble is slowly blown. None of them resemble those from any other country, most being of thin lustred glass, although some are silvered in the conventional way. There are from ten to fifteen blowers in each big factory each with his own specialty. Production of Italian ornaments has steadily increased since 1955 until the last four years when America experienced what is known in the trade as "bad Christmases," due to the energy crisis and the consequent cut-back on holiday lighting and decorations, both in stores and homes. A sales spurt is expected soon as the American exchange rate with Italy now favors increased trade. Italian ornaments have proven so desirable that copies are now being made more cheaply by both Mexican and Colombian glass-blowers in an extensive range of figurals, including angels, Santas, birds, animals, mushrooms and stars. Fortunately the devastating floods in Florence in 1966 did not inundate the ornament works, although many Christmas-lighting factories were severely hit and had to be closed for repairs.

Domestically, Corning Glass and Max Eckardt's Shiny Brite ornaments have dominated the market since the war. One small but growing firm is the old establishment of Krebs und Sohn which opened an

American branch of an old-world factory in Roswell, New Mexico in 1974. Founded by Erika Krebs in Rosenheim, Bavaria, who gained her expertise in Bohemia (Czechoslovakia), the firm is now run by her grandsons. Mostly ball and bell shapes and usually made of pastel lustered glass, they are decorated with paint, embroidery, braid, glitter, tinsel, and occasionally panels of silk depicting scenes of Christmas. All the ornaments have the traditional crown caps of Krebs und Sohn. In 1978, the firm will present its first glass figurals.

The growth of nostalgia gripping America in the late sixties and seventies is evidenced in part by the rekindling of interest in "collectors" items." Collectors' Christmas plates had been made by the Bing and Grondahl factory after 1908, each dated. In the 1970s, manufacturers were turning out scores of dated items—more plates, eggs, sterling silver Christmas ornaments, mugs, bells, plaques, and finally Christmas tree ornaments in glass. Made in limited editions and usually dated by year, they have been big sellers. The "collector's series" ornaments, begun in 1972, are made by a variety of firms, with other concerns controlling the design copyrights (as a general rule). Each ornament is expensive, and older "editions" of the same ornament are correspondingly more expensive, if available. Thus far, all have been ball forms with designs of popular subjects printed on a vinyl sleeve which fits around the ball. The designs are silk-screened onto the vinyl.

"Holly Hobby" appears on many collectors items – cups, plates, dolls, plaques, pillows – and glass Christmas ornaments!

Identifying and Collecting Ornaments

There are many clues which can help identify an ornament. Distinguish first between the old and new ornaments: feel it in the hand. The really old one looks like gossamer; it sounds hollow, brittle, and fragile. The newer ornament appear much heavier and when tapped sounds dull. Judge next the fineness of detail; if it is quite crude it could be Japanese, Polish, or Mexican, for example. Turn the ornament over, and decide whether the back has been finished with the same careful detailing as the front. Old ornaments have carefully molded reverse sides. Frequently the new is less carefully worked, or alternately, too perfectly done. This is especially the case with the painting used to set off details on the ornament. The style of the ornament should establish something about it: Polish birds are larger than others, for example, and Polish balls have a typical pear-shape with a tip on the bottom. Consult the ornament chart for help in determining dates of ornaments. Look for the country of origin on the cap, but beware lest the caps have been replaced or exchanged. If the original box in which the ornaments were shipped is available, examine it for country of origin or name of manufacturer. Finally, the subject matter itself may place an ornament easily. As a simple example, an astronaut-on-the-moon ornament can be pinpointed to the year 1969 exactly.

Sources in Germany report that enthusiasm there for collecting antique ornaments is in the formative stages in contrast to the United States. Emphasis has always been placed on having a beautiful Christmas tree, not on having a tree covered with unique figurals of great value. Apparently the Germans have preferred balls and various geometric shapes when choosing glass ornaments. The search for old ornaments, however, may become more fervent as the "nostalgia boom" (the particular time span that collectors refer to as the "new-old": 1890-1940) spreads Eastward, and they grow to appreciate more fully this small, but significant part of their own culture.

Naturally the value and prices of ornaments are escalating. While collecting ornaments may still be accomplished with relative ease, finding the unusual treasure will soon be difficult, particularly the figurals. The best source is a house sale where boxes of ornaments are usually offered at a low price. Rummage sales and flea markets often yield unexpected bounty. Antique shops command premium prices, but if a rarity turns up, price is no object to the genuine collector. In the United States, both prices and availability of ornaments may vary widely by geographical region. Assuredly marked price increases can be anticipated as more people discover their appeal and fascination. Some collectors find they enjoy collecting the newer Italian and European figurals, and decorate spectacular trees. Others cherish "collector balls." They demonstrate it is never too late to begin an ornament collection!

The authors, Maggie Rogers and Judith Hawkins, looking through but a few of the hundreds of ornaments they checked while choosing those to include in their book.

Like all antiques, Christmas ornaments can represent good investments, not only financially, but spiritually, since they seem to satisfy a longing for the old sense of magic and excitement of Christmas which has prevailed since pagan times. Certainly their frail beauty and inherent charm will continue to delight generations to come.

APPENDIX 1

Repair of Tree Ornaments

All needed materials and bits and pieces of broken ornaments for repair should be kept together in a "shoe box hospital." Materials should include Elmer's glue, toothpicks, tissue paper (colored and white), cotton, sealing wax, cuticle scissors and Testor's model airplane paint (flat white and metallic colors), diamond dust, and assorted tubes of colored sprinkles which come pre-mixed with glue.

Practice first on a small break or hole in an ornament. Apply a band of glue around the opening. Place a piece of tissue paper, slightly larger than the hole, carefully over the hole, and smooth it gently with a toothpick. Next, apply a coat of glue over the entire area, and let it dry completely. Then apply paint of the nearest color available. Use a metallic paint made by Testor's, allowing the silver to remain in the bottom of the jar, using only the lacquer coloring which remains on top. If color matching proves impossible, try to incorporate the color of the mend on the ornament somewhere, if this does not offend your sensibilities. (Some collectors prefer to leave a valuable ornament untouched.) When attempting to repair a larger hole, remove the ornament cap, and tuck some glue-soaked cotton through the hole. Using a long slender stick and working through the cap opening, press the cotton to fill in the hole area. Let it dry. "Prick out" the cotton with a needle to shape it to conform to the contour of the ball. Then apply tissue over the cotton as is done on smaller holes. If the cotton should flatten down, puff it up again with a needle. Apply several coats of metallic lacquer to achieve a strong bond.

Slightly more finesse and patience is required for broken tops and necks due to their contours. Practice first on small breakouts where the metal top will no longer hold, following the same procedure as on bodies. Where there is a contour, as at the base of the neck, clip the tissue paper just as curves are clipped in dressmaking. Dry well before re-inserting tops. When breaks are extensive in this area, carefully build up with tissue, piece by piece, snipping curves to conform to shape, letting each piece dry before applying another. If the entire neck is missing, a new neck can be fashioned by shaping and gluing tissue around a small dowel (smaller than a pencil). When dry, remove, insert in the ornament and glue. Again apply several coats of lacquer as before. It helps to apply a coat of clear lacquer over the cap area and on the neck for strength.

Any missing "snow" effect can be duplicated by painting an area with flat white Testor's paint, and while wet, sprinkling either diamond or glass dust over it. Various colored sprinkles mixed with glue are available on the market to fill or copy an original ornament design. The silvering on the interior of an ornament can only be replaced professionally which is extremely costly.

To replace legs on birds, simply reheat any remaining wax on the leg and re-apply. If no wax remains, drip wax into the socket on the body and replace the leg. Glue works well, but is slower and not as authentic.

Suggestions of

Mrs. Elmer J. Soumie,
  Portland, Oregon

Mr. Harry W. Shuart,
  Suffern, New York
and the authors

APPENDIX 2

Chronology of Caps, Hangers, and Marking Regulations to Aid in Identifying Christmas Ornaments

1. Cork cap, fits into neck of ornament, either a rubber string or twine extending from it.

   kugel/schecken
   1870–1880s

2. Flat, embossed brass cap with attached metal ring (embossed designs taken from old brass curtain tie-backs).

   ca. 1885

3. Clip device in use, as used to clip candles onto tree branch.

   1880s-1977

4. 1st metal tree hook, fitting into cap loop, very successful.

   1892-1977

5. Flat cap of unembossed tin in use.

   1900-1913

6. 1st legislation requiring marking 'country of origin' on all imported goods: McKinley Tariff Act of 1890. Ornaments, though required, remain unmarked due to 1) fragility of ornaments and 2) marking of boxes, not ornaments.

   1890-1932

7. Cap used with two holes, to be threaded with hanging material; untenable.

   ca. 1908

8. Cap comprised of stick with wire attached for hanging, expanded pieces of cardboard suspended inside ornament, fastened to stick. Unsuccessful.

   ca. 1912

9. Cap with built-in spring hook, simple and very successful.

   1913-1977

10. Unidentified American glass-makers marking ornaments "Made in U.S. of A."

    1918-1939

11. Max Eckardt marking ornaments "Made in U.S. of A." Blanks purchased from N.J. glass-makers, finished by his firm; still used in 1977 if ornaments shipped to Canada.

    1920-1937

12. U.S. marking requirements specifically exempt ornaments from labelling provided 'country of origin' shown on box: Smoot-Hawley Tariff Act of 1930.

    in effect
    1932-1937

13. Crown-shaped cap with scalloped edge introduced by Krebs und Sohn, Bavaria Roswell, New Mexico.

    1935-1977

14. Cap marked "Premier" Premier Glass Works, N.J.

    1935-40

15. Corrugated cap, marked "Shiny Brite" trademark of Max Eckardt.

    1937-1977

16. Definitive marking required on cap of 'country of origin' by die sinking or use of string tag or sticker unless ornaments are in window boxes or unless box remains unopened until reaching final customer. Congressional action: Custom Tariff decision #54387.

    1937-1977

17. U.S. war-time cap of rust/gray/ivory/ Kraft paper with paper hanger incorporated into cap. Useful metal substitute.

    1941-1947

18. Scalloped cap marked "Made in U.S.A." on all Corning ornaments although ornaments may be finished products of another company, i.e. George Francke.

    1947-1977

19. "Made in Occupied Japan" marking.

    1947-1951

APPENDIX 3

Countries Making Minor Contributions to the Glass Ornament Industry

1.	Australia	One British firm manufacturing ornaments in Sydney.
2.	Argentina	Ornaments, $6,000 worth of assorted, colored balls, brought in 1946 through Louisiana. Heavy glass.
3.	Belgium	A French company in Belgium made large balls, in various colors, with kugel-like caps and hanging ring. (Glasblozerijen der Schelde N.V.)
4.	Canada	The Canadian Paper Novelty Company made assortment of fancy glass reflectors.
5.	China	Insignificant collection of common balls, assorted sizes, several colors during thirties.
6.	Columbia	Under aegis of Harold Eckardt (son of Max), producing interesting figurals (1970s); has sophisticated machines capable of reproducing any type of old ornament wanted.
7.	Denmark	Jali Papierindustri of Copenhagen makes straw and paper decorations; imports glass ornaments from continent so glass source is uncertain from Denmark.
8.	Finland	K.A. Weiste Oy of Helsinki have made and exported glass ornaments since 1924, mostly to Northern Europe.
9.	France	Very limited production of basket-ball-sized spheres, many colors; kugel caps/rings
10.	Hong Kong	British-owned firms have made ornaments, usually balls, strings of beads (1969-77).
11.	Hungary	Ornaments marked Hungary really Austro-Hungarian (products of Austrian blowers).
12.	India	Unknown; perhaps ornaments were listed as 'glass' having glass-dust or glass beads/sequins as trim.
13.	Israel	Exciting "new" ornaments: glass cars, cigars, etc. Very well done, limited supply.
14.	Korea	Korea has supplanted Japan's production, has taken over much of her work.
15.	Mexico	Largely crude, heavy forms with thorn-like projections; figurals are tear-drop forms with caps forming turbans of 'Three Wise Men.'
16.	Netherlands	A Netherlands Company in The Hague has exported them: no information available.
17.	Romania	Fairly crude work, simple ornaments like teapots.
18.	Spain	"El Carnival" of Barcelona producing good quality ornaments on large scale. Ornaments look Mexican, usually in frosty colors: bells, candy canes of twisted glass, and interesting tear-drop figurals. Knob on top forms the heads of 3 Wise Men, Shepherds, Peasants, 3 Kings, Madonna.
19.	Sweden	Individual glass-makers making unidentified ornaments.
20.	Switzerland	Heavy, clear glass balls with relief work on side, annealed self-hooks of glass. Elegant.

21.	Taiwan	Since 1975, many glass balls, and solid glass icicycles. (Machine-made).
22.	Turkey	No information available as to type of ornament.
23.	United Kingdom	Porth Textiles, Ltd., of Glamorgan, Wales and Glass Balls, Ltd., of Harworth, Doncaster are main suppliers of the Commonwealth.
24.	Yugoslavia	No information available, as to type of ornament.

APPENDIX 4

Collector's Series: All Designs Printed on Vinyl Sleeves Encircling Ball Forms

Company	Design	Dated	1st yr.	Blanks	Copy-right by	Remarks
1. Colby Glass, Woonsocket, Rhode Island	"Baby's 1977 Christ-mas"	Yes	1977	Colby	original art from Spain	First venture into "Collector's Series" field, although firm has been producing ornaments since 1952.
2. Corning Glass, Wells-boro, Pa.	Holly Hobby	1 undated, all Bicen-tennial scenes dated	1975	Corning	Ameri-can Greet-ings, Cleve-land, Ohio	The Gardoc Co., New Hampshire, does all 5-color print-ing for Corning on vinyl sleeves. Draw-ings of Holly Hobby done by a real per-son living in Mass-achusetts, of her own children and child-hood memories.
	Bird Mas-ters (Gold-finch mates) (Chickadee mates) (Cardinal mates)	Yes	1976	Corning	Klips-ringer, N.J.	Series of 6 birds drawn by Chuck Ripper, National Wildlife Federation Artist, 3¼" diameter
	Currier and Ives	1972-5 dated 1976–not dated	1972 (sales test); 1973 to present on market	Corning	public domain	Larger ornaments than Hallmark's of similar design, all 3¼"; featuring in 1976: old Grist Mill, Early Winter, Amer-ican Homestead.
	Drum Collection	No	1973-6	Corning		Drum Collection was packaging concept, designs child-orien-ted: Santa Claus, Mother Goose, religious scenes, toy train, etc.

Company	Design	Dated	1st yr.	Blanks		
	Great Masters: Raffaelo Madonna, Tintoretto Nativity, Leonardo Annunciation	Yes	1976	Corning	public domain	Three ornaments in humidor box featuring great works of art.
3. David Grossman, St. Louis, Mo.	Norman Rockwell scenes	Yes	1975	Corning and G.E. (in 1977, Colby Glass will make all glass ornaments.)	Saturday Evening Post	1976–Santa Claus surrounded by children 1976–Good little boys and girls 1977–Grandpa riding Hobby horse
	Looney Tunes	Yes	1977	Colby	Warner Brothers Hollywood	Characters from movie cartoon of same name.
4. Hallmark Co., Kansas City, Mo.	Currier and Ives	Some, not all. All dated for Bicentennial.	1973	Colby Glass	public domain	Printed by Gardoc Co., New Hampshire, excellent halftones and color reproduction through special 10-color process on vinyl sleeve.
	Norman Rockwell scenes	"		Colby	David Grossman	In 1976/76 Hallmark did own printing.
	Peanuts/ Snoopy		1977	Colby	Determined Products, San Francisco	
5. Natural Designs, St. Louis, Mo.	Norman Rockwell scenes	Yes	1976	Corning and G.E.	David Grossman	Natural Designs is a subsidiary of David Grossman Co., St. Louis. Scenes were the "Four Seasons," 2 5/8" diameter.
6. Schmid Brothers, Randolph, Mass.	Hummels	Yes	1974	Corning	W. Goebel-Porzellantabrik, Rödental, West Germany	Scenes chosen from paintings of Sister Berta Hummel, Franciscan nun, who died in 1935. Each ornament has a matching plate.
	Walt Disney characters	Yes	1974	Corning	Walt Disney Productions	

30

Raggedy Ann	Yes	1976	Corning	Bobbs-Merrill, Indian-apolis
Peter Rabbit scene	Yes	1977	Corning	Freder-ick Warne, New York

APPENDIX 5

A Collector's Guide To Glass Christmas Tree Ornaments

Ornaments listed must, of necessity, be only a representative sampling of major countries involved. Dates listed are times ornaments arrived on the U.S. ornament market. (No notation is made of interruption of ornament imports during World War I: 1915-20; there were virtually none.)

KEY

Manufacturing technique:

F   Free-hand blown (no molds used)
HM   Ornament made in mold while glass being mouth-blown into it.
MM   Glass-blowing process accomplished entirely be machine.
F & HM Part of ornament is mouth-blown without mold, part blown utilizing mold.
B   Ornament is composed of small glass beads, wired into shapes.
NP   No illustration available, but known ornament exists.

Scarcity Ratings

Based on appraisals from the East, Mid-west, and West (U.S.A.). Ratings do not reflect beauty or charm of ornament; only its rarity. 1 rare; 2 scarce; 3 fairly common; 4 common

Countries by Abbreviation

L-S	Lauscha-Steinheid	USA	United States
Aus.	Austria	W.Ger.	Western Zone of Germany
Czech.	Czechoslovakia	E. Ger.	Eastern Zone of Germany
Pol.	Poland		

Note: No ornaments during World War II

Acorns

Mediaeval legends view acorns as new life springing from the Tree of Life.

Category	Type of ornament	Illustration number	Where made	When made	How made	Rarity scale	Price index	General facts
		14A,B	L-S	1870s-1939	HM	3-4	1-10	Various sizes. Usual Lauschan glass, but a few early acorns
		14C	Aus.	1920s-77	HM	3-4	1-5	resemble very early kugels: heavy glass, embossed cap with ring hanger. Some "ODDITY" ornaments which incorporate acorns.
		NP	USA	1939	MM	3-4	5	Made by Corning Glass
		NP	Jap.	1925-35	MM	3-4	1-2	Smaller/heavier than German
		NP	E. Ger.	1952-77	HM	3-4	1-2	Miniatures in addition to standard size.

Animals

Animals were an integral part of the Nativity Scene; they were first used by St. Francis of Assisi around the creche. Many European peasants believed that animals in both stable and forest fell on their knees in adoration on the Christmas Eve Christ was born, and many animals, especially horses and pigs, have human tongues with which to prophecy about the coming year. Many toy animals were made by Thuringian artisans, hand-carved and covered with chamois and fur, which probably served as models for the ornament-makers.

A. DOGS

15 21 B C 28 B L-S	1870-1920s	HM	2	12-18	Often whimsical, seen wearing	
21 A W. Ger.	1950-77	MM	3	2-4	neckties or sitting in purses/ baskets.	
NP Italy	1955-77	F	3-4	4-5	Difficult to distinguish from a bear.	

Variants:
1. Dog in Doghouse	26 L-S	1870s-1920	HM	1	20-25
2. Dog with Basket	NP L-S	1890	HM	1+	35

2. Dog with Basket — Imported to Richmond, Va.; carries golden basket in his mouth.

3. Bulldog Face	23 L-S	1870s-1920	HM	1+	30

3. Bulldog Face — Single dog face rarer than body form.

4. Scotty Dog	29 L-S	1870s-1920	HM	1	15

4. Scotty Dog — Sitting position.

B. CATS

16 L-S	1870-1920s	HM	2	15-20	Appear in shoes, bags, purses,
NP W. Ger.	1950-77	MM	3	2-4	either lying down or peeking out.
NP Italy	1955-77	F	3	5-6	Many varieties: Krazy Kats, alley cats, leopards, etc.

C. SQUIRRELS

3 B L-S	1870-1920s	HM	2	15-18	Several sizes available.
NP W. Ger.	1950-77	MM	3	2-4	Relatively crudely molded.
NP Italy	1955-77	F	3	2-4	Upright squirrel, rearing up like kangaroo, showing his belly.
NP Czech.	1965-67	MM	4	2-4	Similar to West German ones.

D. RABBITS

3 A L-S	1870-1939	HM	2	15-18	Rabbit in sitting position, eating giant carrot, was made as early as 1870 in Steinheid. Rabbits quite similar to squirrels, but have long, pendulous ears.
NP E. Ger.	1967	HM	2	12-15	Used old mold for re-run.
NP Italy	1955-77	F	3	5-6	Have big head, large erect ears, ball-form body.

Variant:
Rabbit Emerging from Egg	18 L-S	1890-1920s	HM	1	35-45

Rabbit Emerging from Egg — Large fantasy period piece.

E. HEDGEHOGS

2 L-S	1870s-1939	HM	1	15-20

F. PIGS

4 34 L-S	1870s-1939	HM	2	15-18	Very few pig ornaments made considering so many made in marzipan.

Variant:
Three Little Pigs	126 L-S	1930s	HM	2	20-25	From childrens' tale: fat, upright
	W. Ger.	1950-77	MM	3	4-6	pigs.
	NP Italy	1955-77	F	3	7-8	Running, legs extended.
	NP E. Ger.	1952-77	HM	2	4-6	Resemble Lauschan pigs.

G. MONKEYS
Said to be modelled after early Italian glass pigs, used as decorative objects around 1875.

28 A L-S	1870s-1939	HM	1-2	8-12	
NP E.Ger.	1952-77	HM	2	3-5	

H. FROGS

20 A B L-S	1870s-1939	HM	2	15-18	Available in 2 positions: crouch-
NP Czech.	1925-39	HM	2	12-15	ing and front-view with exposed
NP W. Ger.	1952-77	MM	3-4	3-4	belly/open mouth. Early frog
20 E. Ger.	1952-77	HM	2	3-4	ornament has frog sitting, strum-ming banjo
NP Aus.	1950-77	HM	3–	3-4	Often see new Austrian frog play-ing banjo.

I. ELEPHANTS

25 L-S	1870s-1939	HM	1	18-20	Comes in various sizes.
NP E. Ger.	1952-77	HM	2	2-3	Small, lustre glass, glitter trim; clip-on.
NP Italy	1955-77	F	3	5-7	Various types: Dumbo, sitting, standing ones.

J. CRABS

Ancient sign of Cancerians.

NP L-S	1870s-1939	HM	1 + +	150-175	Made in 2 pieces: a carapece and ventral shell held together by pin. Moveable.

K. SPIDER-IN-WEB

Old Hungarian tale speaks of spider who wove a web around a poor woman's tree and it turned to silver on Christmas morning. Reputedly initiated idea of tinsel on trees. Spider is good luck symbol of Ukraine.

24 L-S	1870s-1939	HM	1	20-25	Spider in relief on carefully molded web.
NP Czech.	1905-77	B	4 +	2-4	Web outlined in beads.

L. ALLIGATORS

1 L-S	1870s-1939	F	1	50-65	Oldest ornaments are in prone position, clip-on hanger.
NP W. Ger.	late 1950s	F	2	6-8	Alligator standing up.

M. PENGUINS

NP Jap.	1925	MM	1	10-12	Small ornaments: 1½".
19 L-S	1930s	F	2	8-10	Colored glass, unsilvered.

N. BEARS
(conventional types)

5 32 L-S	1870s-1939	HM	1	15-20	Differ from toy Teddy Bears.
NP Aus.	1920s-1977	HM	1	2-15	
NP W. Ger.	1950-77	MM	3	2-4	Many varieties: one is riding motorcycle.
NP Italy	1955-77	F	4	5-7	Wide choice: sitting bears, Pandas, Mama/Papa bears, etc.

Variants:
1. Dancing Bear on Ball

NP L-S	1870s-1939	HM	1+	100-125	
NP E. Ger.	1952-77	HM	1-2	15-20	Re-run in old mold.

2. Bear Carrying Stick
May be modelled after Teddy Roosevelt political logo.

NP L-S	1870s-1939	HM	1+	30-50	

O. OCTOPUS

31 W. Ger.	1950s	F	3-4	5-6	

P. LADYBUGS/BEETLES

17 L-S	1910-39	HM	1	30-40	Soft, lustred finish; indented wing outlines.
NP Czech.	1925-39	HM	2	30-40	
NP Italy	1955-77	F	3	4-6	Painted red/black; stylish, has six legs.

Q. HORSES

NP L-S	1880s	HM	1 + +	150	One horse reportedly made on special order for F.A.O. Schwartz, NYC, with free-standing legs.
30 L-S	1930s	HM	1	40-50	Blue horse, came in a set with blue crane, 2 ducks.

	NP Italy	1955-77	F	3	6-7	Resembles hobby-horse with out rockers; free-standing legs.
Variant: Horse in Bas-relief on Ball-form	22 L-S	1890-1920	HM	2-3	10-12	Usually find horses on ornaments, not as free form.
R. ASSORTED ANIMALS 1. Turtles	NP Italy	1955-77	F	3	4-6	Various colors; shell plaques outlined in glitter.
2. Seal with Ball	NP			2	8-10	White seal, blue ball; clip.
3. Kangaroos	NP			1	5-7	Resembles rabbit; baby in pouch.
4. Lions	NP			3	5-6	Has fur ruff around neck.
5. Tigers	NP			3	4-5	Orange body with black plush stripes.
6. Snails	NP			2	6-8	Pearlescent with glittery antennae.
7. Dinosaurs	NP			2	7-9	Very large, upright.
	33 W.Ger.	early 1950s	F	3-4	8-10	Remarkable piece.

Baskets

Baskets replicated the mode of carrying ornaments and toys, flowers and fruit, to markets and homes in Germany and abroad.

A. CONVENTIONAL VARIETIES FILLED WITH FRUIT/FLOWERS	6 B L-S	1870s-1939	HM	3-4	3-6	Available in many sizes, colors, and shapes.
	36 A Aus.	1920s-77	HM	3-4	1-5	
	NP Czech.	1905-77	B	4	2-4	
	36 B	1925-77	HM	3-4	1-5	
	NP W. Ger.	1950-77	MM	4	1-2	Some new baskets are larger, have flocking trim, fabric flowers.
	NP E. Ger.	1952-77	HM	4	1-2	Also make miniature baskets marked West Germany.
Variants 1. Baskets holding angel	6 A L-S	1870s-1939	HM	1	18-20	
2. Baskets holding fabric flowers/glanzbilder	35 L-S	1870s-1939	HM	2-3	10-12	
3. Basket holding Santa	37 L-S 215 A	1870s-1939	HM	2	18-20	

Bells

Symbol of joyful Christmas season, announcer of tidings, usually good ones. Many old tales surround bells: one favorite repeats that on the night that Christ was born, evil died, and that for one hour that Christmas Eve, bells rang for one hour throughout the world. Tradition also says that the old custom of ringing bells on people's door-steps at Christmas-time (schneckel) was brought to America by immigrants to the Pennsylvania Dutch colony in 1750. Bell choirs became very popular in England beginning in the 17th century, and by the turn of the century in America the handbell had become the common school-room bell.

A. USUAL FORMS 7 8A 44 47 L-S	1868-1939	HM	4	2-5	European bells fragile, have separate glass bead clappers. Bells
48 49 Czech.	1905-77	B	4	2-3	tinkle when sounded. Often have
8 C	1925-77	HM	4	2-5	bas-reliefs on surfaces, trimmed
8 B Aus.	1920s-77	HM	4	2-5	with snow, glass beads, glanzbilder, painting or combinations of above. Some miniatures.
NP Jap.	1920s-41	MM	3-4	1-3	Japanese bells crude, heavy with strong colors. Many miniatures. No separate clappers.

	No.	Origin	Dates	Mat.			Notes
	46	W. Ger.	1950-77	MM	4	1-5	Newer European bells heavier, lack fine detailed finishing. Most have separate clappers; some have molded clappers.
	NP	E. Ger.	1952-77	HM	3	1-5	Also make miniatures.
	NP	USA	1939-40	MM	3	10	Corning made bells for short time only.
	43		1939-77	MM	4	1-2	"Shiny Brite" bells by Max Echardt
	NP		1939-77	MM	4	1-2	George Francke bells.
	NP		1952-77	MM	4	1-2	Colby Glass bells. American bells relatively heavy, usually no separate clappers. Decorated with snow/painting.
	NP	Italy	1955-77	F	3	3-4	Most are large and lightweight.
	192 A	USA	1974-77	MM	4	1-4	Krebs und Sohn, New Mexico., largely pale colors, usually with separate clappers, wide variety of trim: braid, silk panels, etc. Various sizes.
B. HANDBELLS	Stein 9 heid		1870s-1939	HM	2-3	8-10	Pike on ornament forms the handle. See also ROYALTY ITEMS
	45	Aus.	1920s-77	HM	3-4	8-10	
	NP	W. Ger.	1950-77	MM	4	1-3	Roughly finished.

Birds

Birds, symbolic of spiritualization, have long been considered eloquent messengers of God and love. Bird ornaments are the most common figurals, being close companions of all trees.

	No.	Origin	Dates	Mat.			Notes
A. COMMON SONG BIRDS	39 62	L-S	1870s-1939	FHM	4	3-7	Usually have spun glass or crinkly wire tail. Hung initially from annealed glass hook on body. Later used clips/coiled metal legs fitting into indentations on bird's belly, held by wax. May find two birds on one clip. Rare bird has paper/spun glass wings.
	NP	Czech.	1905-77	B	4	2-4	Outlines of birds.
	39 40 58	Czech.	1925-77	FHM	4	3-7	Czech birds either very large or very small; frequently have wire filaments encasing them or wire wings/tail.
	39	Aus.	1920s-77	FHM	4	3-7	Similar to German birds.
	42	Jap.	1920s-39	MM	3	2-5	Occasionally look like balls joined to make a bird, with details added on.
	NP	W. Ger.	1950-77	MM	4	1-2	
	NP	E. Ger.	1952-77	FHM	4	1-2	
	NP	USA	± 1965	MM	4	1	Made for Shiny Brite in Japan.
B. OWLS Symbol of wisdom, popular motif of early 20th C.	12 60	L-S	1870s-1939	HM	2	4-8	Most owls have clip-on hangers; some have spun glass tails, more common ones do not.
	60 A	Czech.	1925-77	HM	2	4-8	
	12 B 60 C	Aus.	1920s-77	HM	2	4-8	
	NP	W. Ger.	1950-77	MM	3-4	1-2	Good copies of old owl ornaments since WWII, frequently hard to distinguish from old.
	NP	E. Ger.	1952-77	HM	2	2-4	
C. PARROTS/COCKATOOS/PARAKEETS Considered objects of great beauty/rarity since Biblical times.	10 55	L-S	1870s-1939	FHM	2-3	10-12	Colorful plumage alluring; majority of ornaments silvered, but some (old and new) finished in matte paint only. Birds frequently sit in wire or tinsel rings.
	55	Czech.	1925-77	FHM	2-3	10-12	

	NP W. Ger.	1950-77	MM	3-4	1-3	New parrots lack rings.
	NP E. Ger.	1952-77	FHM	2-3	1-3	
D. STORKS	38 63 L-S	1870s-1920	F	1	15-20	Few perfect examples remain of old storks due to fragility of long
Variant: Mother/Baby Stork	59 A L-S	1870s-1920	F	1+	25-30	legs/beak which are annealed onto body.
	NP W. Ger.	1950-77	F	2	2-4	
	NP E. Ger.	1952-77	F	1	2-4	
	NP Italy	1955-77	F	1	5-7	White glass, fat body, long beak/legs.
E. GOLDFINCHES	NP L-S	1870s-1939	FHM	2	3-7	Sometimes paired on clip.
F. TURKEYS (animal form)	59 B L-S	1870s-1939	HM	2	4-10	Usually seen as bas-reliefs on "House" ornaments, in front or side yards. Animal form is much more unusual.
	NP W. Ger.	1952-77	MM	2	1-2	
G. PASSENGER PIGEONS	NP L-S	1890-1920	FHM	1	15-20	Mold broken, no longer made.
H. PEACOCKS Symbol of vanity and pride.	13 L-S	1870s-1939	HM	2-3	6-12	Soft lustre finish on old ornament; muted painting as trim. Various poses, sizes.
	61 A Czech.	1965-77	HM	3	2-4	Highly silvered, brightly painted, wear small golden crown.
I. BLUE-WINGED CRANES	41 L-S	1930s	F	1	10	Came in set with blue horse and 2 ducks. Similar to stork, fragile but not large.
J. SWANS Long sacred to Venus and Aphrodite, symbols of beauty and purity.	61 C L-S	1870s-1939	HM	1	15-20	
	NP Aus.	1920s-1939	HM	1-2	25	Only one swan reported in Austrian ornament literature.
	NP Czech.	1967-77	HM	2	2-4	Czechoslovakians usually incorporate wire into design around ornament.
	NP Italy	1955-77	F	1	4-6	Made of white frosted glass with painted eyes; fat.
K. HUMMINGBIRDS	59 C L-S	1870s-1939	FHM	1	3-7	Occasionally find two birds on single clip; occasionally trimmed with glass beads. Generally tiny birds.
	NP W. Ger.	1950-77	MM	3	2-3	
L. DUCKS	27 L-S	1870s-1939	HM	2	8-10	Painted bill.
	NP Italy	1955-77	F	4	4-5	Donald Duck, conventional types, etc.
M. PELICANS	11 L-S	1870-1920s	HM	1	15-18	
	NP Jap.	1920s-39	MM	1	10-12	
N. FLAMINGOES	61 B L-S	1870-1920s	FHM	1	20	Delicate neck and long bill exhibits careful workmanship.
O. BIRDS IN NESTS	56 57 L-S	1870s-1939	FHM	1	20	Nest is glass as well as mother/baby birds.
	NP W. Ger.	1950-77	FHM	2	3-5	New nest ornament has nest of angel hair (spun glass), mother/baby sitting on it. Clip on bottom. (Looks like sparrow on nest).

	NP Italy	1955-77	F	3	5-7	Italian version has glass bird with wire wrapped around it. Odd; plastic clip.

P. ASSORTED BIRDS

NP Italy	1955-77	F	2-3	5-7	Italian birds rounded, tubular forms, stylized replicas of birds; lightweight glass, lustred finish.

Q. BIRD AND THOR FACE 202 203

See: ODDITIES

Bird in Birdhouses/ Birdcages

These ornaments have long symbolized the sanctity of the happy home.

50 L-S	1870s-1939	HM	2	5-10	Some birdhouses have embossed ladders leading to opening in
NP Czech.	1946-77	HM	2	2-6	house; a variety of birds seen, in bas-relief on side.
NP W. Ger.	1976	MM	4	2-5	Made of clear glass, trimmed in gold paint.

Butterflies

Butterflies are the emblems of the soul and common design motifs of the Art Nouveau period, late 19th century.

A. BUTTERFLIES, ACTUAL BODY FORM

64B L-S	1870s-1939	F	1-2	20-25	Feature delicate spun-glass wings (pale colors), glued onto body
64C Aus.	1920s-1939	F	1-2	15-20	using fabric tape; glass antennae
64A Czech.	1925-39	F	1-2	15-20	and annealed glass hook as hanger.

B. BUTTERFLIES, GENERALIZED BODY FORM

65A L-S	1870s-1939	HM	2	6-8	Contours of ornament suggest
NP Aus.	1920s-39	HM	2	5-7	body and wings.
NP E. Ger.	1975	HM	3	4-5	Almost iridescent, very detailed molding; blue/green/purple/pink. Lovely. Contours conform to butterfly shape.

C. GLASS ORNAMENTS WITH EMBOSSED BUTTERFLY

65B,C L-S	1870s-1939	HM	2	3-4	Basic form may be ball or other irregular shape.

Circus Ornaments

The hey-day of the American circus was between 1840 and 1920. Clowns, since early Greek and Roman times, were the symbol of simple, sometimes coarse humor and buffonery. Clowns enjoyed their greatest popularity at the turn of the century. Jesters, on the other hand, represented Punch and Judy in the favorite English children's shows. In ancient times jesters were acrobatic mimics who entertained royalty. The Ringmaster of the circus co-ordinated the various acts of the clowns and animals, and was represented both in toys and ornaments. A beloved feature of any circus was the carousel or merry-go-round, which was also a favorite children's toy of this period.

A. CLOWNS

51, 54B, 67, 69, 82B,C L-S	1870s-1939	HM	2	15-18	Occasionally find torso forms, but usually full-bodied without feet.
54A Aus.	1920s-39	HM	2	12-15	Exhibit wide spectrum of facial expressions. Available in many colors.

	54C, 82A W. Ger.	1950-77		4	2-4	Modern clown ornaments hastily colored, little detail. Rarer two-faced clown available.
	NP Italy	1955-77	F	3	6-7	Italian clowns grotesque, ugly. Rather large. Flamboyant painting.
	NP E. Ger.	1952-77	HM	2	2-4	
B. JESTERS	68, 53 L-S	1870s-1939	HM	1	18-20	Jester ornament has typical pointed hat, bells; may/may not show traditional tasseled scepter.
C. HARLEQUINS	52 Italy	1955-77	F	2-3	6-8	Has customary black mask, shaved head, diamond-patterned costume. No old harlequin ornaments made.
D. RINGMASTERS	66 L-S	1870s-1939	F	1	25-30	Resembles Schoenhut toy ringmaster. Glass eyes replaced in illustration. Features paper hat, curly glass wool hair, innovation at turn of the century.
E. CAROUSELS	81A,C L-S	1870s-1939	HM	2	10-12	Various sizes and patterns available.
	81B Czech.	1925-77	HM	2	2-8	Newer carousel ornaments poorly molded, difficult to distinguish figures on them.

Cones

Cones are sacred symbols of motherhood and fertility; unopened cones represent virginity. Old legend from Harz Mountain regions tells of an impoverished family with an ailing father who went in search of fuel one wintry day. An old imp directed them to the best cones. As they filled their baskets, they grew heavier and heavier. When they looked again at the cones, they had turned to silver which is supposedly why early cones were painted silver to be used as decorations on a Christmas tree.

A. REGULAR CONE FORMS Cones may be first figurals blown into cookie molds.	84B L-S	1867-1939	HM	4	2-5	Many sizes and colors, usually pine cones. Most frequent trim is white paint and diamond dust.
	NP Czech.	1905-77	B	4	2-4	
		1925-77	HM	4	1-4	
	NP Aus.	1920s-77	HM	4	1-4	
	NP Jap.	1920-41	MM	4	1-2	
	NP W. Ger.	1950-77	MM	4	1-5	
	NP E. Ger.	1952-77	HM	4	1-5	Miniature cones as well as standard sizes; some very subtly colored in various hues. Large and small forms.
	NP USA	1939-40	MM	2-3	5	Corning made cones in common form, many colors.
Variants:						
1. Finger Cones	83 L-S	1870s-1939	HM	1-2	7	Unusual bent cone of white pine tree.
2. Fir Cones	70 L-S	1920-23	HM	1	10	Rare cone is long, slender, gently curved.
3. Cones with Santa	84A L-S	1925-40	HM	1	10-12	Personages incorporated into side of cone ornaments are charming innovation of this period.
Variant: Japanese face	71 Jap.	1920-39	MM	1	8-10	
4. Cones with Angel	NP L-S	1920-35	HM	1	10-15	
5. Cones with Clown	NP L-S	1920-35	HM	1	10-15	
6. Cones with Indian	47C L-S	1920-35	HM	1	20-25	See INDIANS.

Crosses

Cross stands for salvation, also symbolizes the Tree of Life (the realm of human existence).

NP L-S	1870s-1910	HM	1	15-20	May have embossed designs on
NP Czech.	1905-35	HM	1	15-20	them.

Doll's Heads

Doll is representative of a child, symbol of the future. Many dolls produced by toymakers from Lauschan and Nürmberg area. Both ornament and doll heads feature glass eyes, speciality of Lauschan glass-blowers. Glass doll heads appear as glass baby rattle ornaments, as well.

A. PREMIUM HEADS
Said to be modelled after head of Baby Jesus.

73B L-S	1870-1939	HM	1	35-50	Head is very large, silver-white, lustre finish, with facial details painted on.

B. SMALLER, STANDARD TYPE HEADS
73A,C, 85, 86

72, L-S	1870s-1939	HM	2	25-30	Heads have painted complexions, expressive features, and glass eyes (usually). Some eyes are missing or have been replaced by beads. Reverse sides of heads lack detail. (Also see TOYS)

Fish

The letters of the word form the notarikon of the Greek phrase, Icthus – Jesus Christ, Son of God, Savior: Iesus Christos THeou Uios Soter, thus the fish is the symbol of Christ.

A. COMMON VARIETY GOLDFISH
1. Small goldfish

B. EXOTIC FISH

C. SHARKS

D. FISH

74, 87A L-S	1870s-1939	HM	3	18-20	Rainbow coloring. Fish often have spun glass tail. May incorporate body movement into design. Newer fish much heavier, lack delicate coloring.
147C Aus.	1920s-77	HM	3	2-18	
NP Czech.	1929-39	HM	2	6-8	
	1946-77	HM	3	2-4	
NP W. Ger.	1950-77	MM	4	2-4	
NP E. Ger.	1952-77	MM	3-4	2-4	
87B Jap.	1920s-41	MM	2	10-12	Heavy silvered glass; shark undulates, has crude mold marks.
NP Italy	1955-77	F	3	5-6	Typical Italian-style, flashy.

Flowers

Flowers have been recognized as symbols of beauty since pagan times when frequent offerings were made to Flora, Goddess of Spring.

A. ROSES
Arabian tale repeats that all the rose bushes in the world bloomed the night that Christ was born, and that the rose is Mary's special flower. Rose is old German symbol of *CHRISTKIND*.

B. LOTUS PODS

75A L-S	1870s-1939	HM	2	6-10	Most common of all flower ornaments, available in various sizes, colors, shapes, all very beautiful. Some roses have beaded finish. Early rose has metal cap/ring for hanger.
75C Aus.	1920s-77	HM	3	3-7	
NP W. Ger.	1950-77	MM	4	2-4	Colors are more gaudy, daring.
76B L-S	1870s-1939	HM	1	12-15	
NP Aus.	1920s-77	HM	1	3-12	
NP W. Ger.	1970s	MM	3	2-4	Much larger than Lauschan variety.

C. TRUMPET FLOWERS	76A L-S	1870s-1939	F	1	12-15	Some collectors call these "morning glories." Have sandy finish, delicate shading.
	NP Aus.	1920s-39	F	1	10-12	
D. DAISIES	88A L-S	1870s-1939	HM	1	3-10	More small daisy ornaments exist than large ones.
	NP Aus.	1920s-39	HM	1	3-7	
	NP W. Ger.	1950-77	MM	3	2-4	
E. WHIMSY BLOOMS: "Padulas"	88B L-S	1870s-1939	HM	1	12-15	Fantasy flowers to delight glass-blowers' imagination
	88C Aus.	1920s-39	HM	1	8-12	
F. CALLA LILIES Popularized by Fannie Hurst, authoress (1889-1968), who always wore a sterling silver lily brooch on her dress.	77 L-S	1870s-1939	F	1+	35-45	Very large ornament with thread-wrapped wire stamens
G. TULIPS	75B Aus.	1920s-1939	HM	1	8-10	

Fruit

Fruit represented the "sweetness of Christ's salvation to man." Fruit ornaments were not silvered internally until the late 1920s; before then all fruit ornaments were made of clear, colored glass, with paint trim.

A. APPLES Fruit of the Paradise Tree; symbol of Venus, goddess of love/lovers. Apples used early, gilded, on Christmas trees with other fruits/nuts.	63 L-S	1870s-1939	F	2	2-20	Often has fabric leaves. Also see PARADISE PLAY FIGURES.
	NP W. Ger.	1960s	F	3-4	1-2	Yellow apple, relatively heavy glass.
B. BANANAS	89 L-S	1870s-1920	F	1	8-12	Two sizes: small/large.
C. BERRIES	90A, 96A L-S	1870s-1939	HM	3	1-4	Berries seen as molded fruit, also in bas-relief on balls, other geometric shapes.
	97A Aus.	1920s-77	HM	3	1-3	
	97B Czech.	1925-77	HM	3	1-3	
	NP W. Ger.	1950-77	MM	4	1-2	
	NP E. Ger.	1952-77	HM	3	1-2	
D. CHERRIES	NP L-S	1870-1939	F	2	2-5	Essentially bead forms with occasional attached leaves; also in relief on other shapes.
E. GRAPES	90B, 96B,C L-S	1870s-1939	HM	3-4	1-8	Most popular fruit ornament, usually molded as a unit of individual grapes; various sizes.
	80 USA	ca. 1880-?	HM	1+	25-40	Much controversy over this early, kugel-like grape; see TEXT. Heavy grapes, cap of embossed brass circle/ring. Available in deep purple, cobalt, silver, green, gold. No red. Largest bunch is 10", smallest is 4".
	78C Czech.	1925-77	HM	3-4	1-6	May be decorated with "frost."
	NP W. Ger.	1950-77	MM	4	1-3	Some decorated with "sugar."
	NP E. Ger.	1952-77	HM	3-4	1-3	
F. ORANGES Gilded orange popular on Christmas trees in 19th C.	92 L-S	1870-1920s	F	2-3	6-8	

40

G. PEARS

	79A L-S	1870s-1939	F	2-3	6-9	Newer pears silvered in conventional way, older merely painted, some blushing. Some covered completely with glass beads.
	NP USA	ca. 1880s-?	HM	1+	25-30	Resemble kugel-like grapes of early Pennsylvania Dutch makers.
	NP W. Ger.	1948-77	F	3	1-2	Silvered, gold with green overtones, various sizes.
Variant: Pear with Candle-Holder	94 L-S	1870-1920s	F	1	12-15	Has candle cup on top; subtle painting.

H. PLUMS

	93 L-S	1870s-1939	F	2	5-7	
	NP W.Ger.	1950-77	F	3	2-4	Made by the now defunct Lanissa Company.

I. STRAWBERRIES

78A, 90C, 95, 97C L-S		1870s-1920	HM	2	5-7	Early ones not silvered, painted in matte tones.
	NP E. Ger.	1952-77	HM	2	2-3	Miniature strawberries.

J. WATERMELONS

	78B L-S	1870-1920s	HM	1	15-18	Large, seeds in bas-relief.

K. LEMONS

	91A L-S	1870-1920s	F	2	5-6	None silvered, all painted yellow, dimpled skin.

L. KUMQUATS

	91B L-S	1870-1920s	F	2	3-4	Good coloring.

M. PEACHES

	79C L-S	1870-1920s	F	2	7-8	Delicate tinting.

Guns

Guns created after toy-makers produced best-selling toy guns following American Civil War and Franco-Russian war of 1870. Guns remained very popular during period of Spanish-American war (1898) and Russo-Japanese war (1905).

Only glass pistol ornaments, copied from toy capgun (no rifles, etc.)	98 L-S	1880s-1939	HM	1	30-35	Subtle coloring on gun. Rare ornament is gun in holster (not pictured)

Hearts

Heart remains symbol of love and lovers, the seat of the soul. Motif used especially by the Austrians.

100, 101A,C L-S		1870s-1939	HM	2-3	7-10	Frequently embossed or indented or feature bas-reliefs on surface; may be painted or trimmed with glitter, etc.
	99 Aus.	1920s-77	HM	2-3	2-15	Most detailed, artistic hearts from Austria.
	NP Jap.	1920s-41	MM	2	3-4	Typical heavy glass, crude colors.
	101B W. Ger.	1950-77	MM	4	2-4	Have miniatures as well as standard sizes; miniatures usually marked West Germany although East German-made.
	NP (E.Ger.)	1952-77	HM	2-3	1-2	

Household Objects

A. PIPES

1. Straight	102 L-S	1870s-1939	F	4	3-7	May appear in various shapes long or short-stemmed. Sometimes embellished with berries, vines, flowers, and leaves; older ones usually more elaborate.
	102 Aus.	1920s-77	F		3-7	
2. Classic Bent Dublin	102 Czech.	1925-77	F	2	2-4	
	NP E. Ger.	1952-77	F	2	2-4	

B. PURSES

Item	No./Origin	Dates	Method	Qty	Price	Notes
	127 L-S	1880s-1939	HM	2	12-15	
	NP Aus.	1920s-77	HM	2	3-10	
	NP W. Ger.	1950-77	MM	3	3-5	
	NP E. Ger.	1952-77	HM	2	3-5	

C. PARASOLS& UMBRELLAS
Victorian fashion accessory, utilitarian object.

Item	No./Origin	Dates	Method	Qty	Price	Notes
	103, 114, 124 L-S	1870s-1939	F	2	15-20	Pike forms handle of umbrella ornament; some have crinkly wire, glanzbilder as trim. Both open/closed types.
	NP Czech.	1946-77	F	3	3-6	
	NP W. Ger.	1950-77	F	3	3-6	New ones lack fragility.
	NP Italy	1955-77	F	3	3-5	Italian ornaments have gold braid around rim of umbrella.

D. CLOCKS
Copies of German cuckoo clocks.

Item	No./Origin	Dates	Method	Qty	Price	Notes
	110B L-S	1870s-1939	HM	2	12-15	Old clocks have glanzbilder faces, new ones are crudely molded with careless painting of numerals on face.
	110A Aus.	1920s-77	HM	2-3	2-12	
	NP Czech.	1925-77	HM	2-3	2-12	
	110C W. Ger.	1950-77	MM	3	1-3	

E. HOUSEHOLD UTENSILS
1. Coffee pots
  a. Large pot
2. Tea Pots
3. Sugar Bowls

Item	No./Origin	Dates	Method	Qty	Price	Notes
	109A,C L-S	1870s-1939	HM	3	3-10	Spouts, handles are annealed onto pot bodies; delicate. A few newer pots/bowls have metallic-painted lids.
	NP L-S	1870s-1939	HM	2	10-12	
	109B Czech.	1925-77	HM	3	2-8	
	NP W. Ger.	1950-77	MM	3	1-3	
	NP E. Ger.	1952-77	HM	3	1-3	

4. Tea Pots

Item	No./Origin	Dates	Method	Qty	Price	Notes
	NP Italy	1955-77	F	3	2-4	Resemble usual pots except for lustred-glass.

F. WINE CASKS
(Barrels)

Item	No./Origin	Dates	Method	Qty	Price	Notes
	107A,C L-S	1870s-1939	HM	2	5-7	Early Lauschan ones smaller than modern West German variety, in general: between 2-2½" long.
	107B W. Ger.	1950-77	MM	4	1-3	

G. LANTERNS
Old German gnome figurines seen carrying lanterns similar to ornaments.

Item	No./Origin	Dates	Method	Qty	Price	Notes
	115A,C L-S	1870s-1939	HM	4	3-5	Old-fashioned lanterns with flat sides. Rumored that Polish made a lantern ornament; unverified.
	106B Aus.	1920s-77	HM	4	1-3	
	NP Jap.	1920s-41	MM	3-	1-2	
	NP Czech.	1925-77	HM	4	1-3	
	106A, 115B USA	1939-77	MM	3-	2-4	Made by Corning Glass, George Francke Company, Shiny Brite.
	NP W. Ger.	1950-77	MM	4	1-2	
	NP E. Ger.	1952-77	HM	3	1-3	
	NP Italy	1955-77	F	3	2-4	

H. SHOES
Reflect quite specifically styles of the times.

1. Early Period

Item	No./Origin	Dates	Method	Qty	Price	Notes
	104 L-S	1870s-1915	HM	2	10-15	Early period ornaments copied from Dutch/northern German wooden shoes.

2. Shoe with Kitten

Item	No./Origin	Dates	Method	Qty	Price	Notes
	164A,C L-S	1870s-1915	HM	2	10-12	
	NP Czech.	1925-77	HM	1	4-15	

3. High Heel Woman's Shoe

Item	No./Origin	Dates	Method	Qty	Price	Notes
	NP Lauscha only	1925-38	HM	1	25	Made of colored glass only, not silvered/painted, called "Cinderellas."

4. Saddle Shoe

Item	No./Origin	Dates	Method	Qty	Price	Notes
	113 W. Ger.	1950-77	MM	3	3-5	Quite large, red/green, "saddles" still in vogue in 1950s.

I. BOOTS
Santa Claus symbols as well as traditional footwear

Item	No./Origin	Dates	Method	Qty	Price	Notes
	NP L-S	1870s-1939	HM	2	8-12	Various sizes.
	NP W. Ger.	1950-77	MM	3	1-3	New German boot ornament is heavy, trimmed with gold glitter; Austrian is smaller with plastic cap.
	NP Aus.	1974-77	HM	3-4	1-3	

J. CANDELABRA	NP Czech.	1905-77	B	4	2-5	No known blown-glass candlelabra although they appear in bas-relief on ball/other geometrically-shaped forms.
K. BOTTLES						
1. Wine Bottle	108 L-S	1870s-1939	HM	2	10-15	Have small paper labels.
2. Champagne Bottle in Bucket	NP W. Ger.	1950-77	MM	4	1-2	Ornament dated '75, carelessly finished.
	NP E. Ger.	1972-77	HM	2	3-6	
L. CANDLES	123C Czech.	ca. 1920	F	2	5-7	Heavy silver glass, clear glass wick, fit into metal clips.
	NP Czech.	1905-77	B	4	2-4	Flat outline of candle and saucer.
	NP W. Ger.	1975-77	MM	4	2-3	Glass candle in glass holder.
M. BEER STEINS	NP L-S	1870s-1939	HM	1-2	20	
N. SCISSORS	NP Stein-heid	ca. 1910-1913-14	HM	1-2	25-30	
O. STOCKINGS Their use derives from old St. Nicholas legend.	105 L—S	1890s	HM	1	20	Some stockings filled with toys: see STOCKING under PATRIOTIC ITEMS.
	112 Czech.	1905-77	B	4	2-4	Czech stocking flat outline.
	NP W. Ger.	1950-77	MM	4	1-4	Very large, heavy ornament filled with toys.
P. CHRISTMAS WREATHES Circle of evergreens symbol of eternal life.	NP L-S	1890s-1920	HM	1	15-20	
Q. BALLS OF YARN	123B L-S	1890s-1920	HM	1	15-18	Fantasy period piece.
R. FLAGONS OF END-OF-DAY GLASS Modelled after genuine article; colors vary, also exist in ball forms.	123A L-S	1900-20	F	1	30-35	"End of day" effect also seen in ball form, other shapes.
S. DICE	111 L-S	1880-1930s	HM	2	8-10	Found in various colors.
	NP W.Ger.	1950s	HM	2-3	6-8	Made for short period only.

Houses and Churches

Houses and churches made of wood and paper pulp in the 19th century served as pastille burners (little aromatic briquets impregnated with perfume were lit and smoldered slowly). These were in great demand, and undoubtably served as models for ornament-makers.

Most houses simple cottages which artisans themselves inhabited. Few impressive churches.	118, 119 L-S	1870s-1939	HM	3-4	3-7	Cottages often have turkeys and fences embossed on sides of ornament.
	117 Czech.	1905-39	B	4	2-4	Czech. beaded houses/churches both in flat and 3-dimensional forms. May include rods and different colored bead shapes in ornament.
	116, 179B	1925-39	HM	3-4	3-7	Difficult to distinguish from German.
	NP Czech.	1946-77	HM	4	2-4	
	177A Aus.	1920s-77	HM	3-4	2-4	Old Austrian house ornaments smaller than other newer ones (2"). New ones often trimmed in glitter.

NP	W. Ger.	1950-77	MM	4	1-3	May have glitter-trim, lustre-look to glass.
NP	E. Ger.	1952-77	HM	3-4	1-3	

The Hunt

Hunting, as sport, originated in England in the middle 1700s, was brought to America by Colonial settlers in Virginia, Maryland, and Pennsylvania. Fox hunting was very popular on the Continent as well.

A. FOX HEADS

128B L-S	1870s-1920	HM	1	25-30	

B. STAGS
Earliest stags were made of milk glass in Steinheid, 1875.

128A L-S	1905-30	F	3	6-8	Glass reindeer have a stand incorporated onto body, can rest on tree branch or be used as table decoration.
NP Italy	1955-77	F	3	4-6	Soft gold color ornament, white spots on back, delicate legs.
NP W. Ger.	1970s	F	3	2-3	

C. HORNS
Used in hunt to call dogs, summon hunters, announce trail, quarry, and signal the kill.

125 L-S	1870-1920	F	1	40-45	Hunting horn ornament is primitive form with tinsel hanging string, decorative silk bow. Very large ornament.

Icicles

Symbolic of Winter, extremely popular ornament form. Europeans prefer solid, twisted type. Some collectors believe icicles first ornaments made; earliest known made by Greiner family in 1840. However, not made for commercial use until 1860.

			Solid: 3; double solid: 1-2	colored solid: 1-2; blown: 2		
120, 121 L-S	1860-39	F+S			2-4	First icicles were solid pieces of clear, twisted glass, occasionally as long as 7". Some doubles made. Rarer solid icicles of red, green, or amber color. All have annealed hook on end. Later variety hollow, twisted, usually silvered inside (Some clear with tinsel in interior. Blown type sometimes decorated with colors, rarer one is multicolored.
120, 121 Czech.	1925-77	F+S			2-5	
120, 121 Aus.	1920s-77	F+S			2-5	
NP W. Ger.	1950-77	F+S			1-3	
NP E. Ger.	1952-77	F+S			1-3	
NP Jap.	1965-77	F+S			1	
NP Taiwan	1968-77	S			1	

Indians

The Indian has long been a heroic figure to Americans and a source of extensive legend. They have played a vital, colorful role in US history from the 18th century to present day, and were an integral part of the "Wild West" which fascinated millions.

A. STANDARD VERSIONS
(Face/headdress)

130B L-S	1870s-1939	HM	2	20-25	Only Lauschans and East Germans have Indian molds; this version model for new Indian ornament. Meticulously detailed, authentic ethnic coloring. All Indian ornaments well-finished on obverse and reverse sides.
NP E. Ger.	1952-77	HM	3	2-4	New head garishly-painted, poorly molded, little detail on backside of ornament.

B. INDIAN ON CONES

129C L-S	1870s-1939	HM	1	20-25	

C. INDIAN IN CANOES	130B L-S	1870s-1939	HM	1	35-40	
D. INDIAN BUSTS	129B L-S	1870s-1939	HM	1	25-30	Difficult to make.
E. SMALL INDIAN HEADS	129A L-S	1870s-1939	HM	1	25-30	Has clip on bottom.
F. ESKIMO INDIANS	NP Italy	1955-77	F	3	6-7	Typical tubular form of Italian ornaments; has hood and coat timmed with white fur.
G. INDIANS, STANDING FIGURE	NP Italy	1955-77	F	3	6-7	Has real feather in back of head.

Infancy Items

Infancy ornaments probably were copied from bisque snow-baby figurines, sentimentalized presentations of sweet Victorian children. Snow babies were first made in sugar (tannenbaum confekt) for tree decorations in the early 19th century; later made in bisque, they were most popular between 1906-10. In any form, they are known as "zucker puppen" (sugar dolls) in Germany. It may also be that these baby ornaments are merely representations of babies in general.

Baby playthings appearing as tree ornaments mirrored latest new items for the baby trade.

A. BABIES						
1. Snow-baby in Bunting	152 L-S	1880-1920s	HM	1	20-25	
2. Baby in bunting with pacifier in mouth.	150B L-S	1880-1920s	HM	1	25-30	
3. Baby in bathtub	133 L-S	1890s-1900	HM	1	35-40	Assuredly a "fantasy" period piece.
4. Small Boy on sled	131, 132 L-S	1890-1920s			30-35	Sled is highly detailed on reverse.
B. BABY TOYS						
1. Baby rattle ornament Tin rattles were a Christmas catalogue offering in 1880.	134, L-S 151, 152	1880s-1900	F	2	5-15	Rattle ornament simple; pike left on ball form, pebbles inserted into rattle end.
2. Pacifier ornament First baby teether appeared on market in late 1880s, early 1890s.	122 L-S	1890-1920s	HM	1	10-12	
	150A Czech.	1905-39	B	2	8-10	3-dimensional.

Lamps
Standing/Table

Edison's patents in 1879, revolutionized lighting throughout the world; this was reflected in the creation of glass lamp ornaments. Lamp shades were made of many different materials, including milk glass, which reached the zenith of its appeal between 1870 and 1880.

153B,C, 154 L-S	1870s-1939	F	2	15-20	Shades of ornaments often trimmed with lacy gold paper or painted designs. Occasionally they simi-late milk glass, had fluted edges.
153A Czech.	1946-77	F	2	8-10	
NP W. Ger.	1950-77	F	3	2-5	
NP E. Ger.	1952-77	F	2	2-5	
NP Italy	1955-77	F	3	3-5	Italian lamps garishly colored, offered with various shade shapes.

Man-in-the-Moon Ornaments

Many myths surround the ornament: early Biblical reference (Numbers 15:32-36) states "man" is being punished for picking up sticks on Sabbath. Early Greeks thought he was frightening apparition who kept evil from moon, residence of the sun god. Another legend reports sun was in love with his sister, the moon, and to escape his cloying attention, she went out only at night with face disguised by ugly smears. Other tales relate that man-in-the-moon, the bad counterpart of Father Christmas, (who carries switches), is a later-day impersonation of Saturn who ate his own children. Still another Bohemian tale declares that a bogeyman lives in the moon who eats bad girls and boys before Christmas.

135 L-S	1870s-39	HM	1	25-35	Large, silvered-glass form with painted features or a bas-relief face on spherical form.
NP Czech.	1946-77	HM	1	3-5	
NP Aus.	1947-77	HM	2	3-10	Two types: usual silvered and clear glass with metallic gold trim.
NP W. Ger.	1950-77	MM	3	2-3	New German ornament of clear or white glass with painted features (red/blue)
NP Italy	1955-77	F	3	5-7	Various types, man usually separate figure glued onto moon.

Musical Instruments

A. VIOLINS
Toy violins very popular.

161B L-S	1870s-1939	HM	2	8-10	No wire on ornament.
NP Aus.	1920s-39	HM	2	6-8	Contemporary Austrian violins
	1947-77	HM	3	2-4	are small.
NP Czech.	1925-77	HM	2	2-6	
NP W. Ger.	1950-77	MM	4	2-3	Some have crinkly wire.
NP E. Ger.	1952-77	HM	2	2-3	

B. CELLOS

156A L-S	1870s-1939	HM	2	8-10	
NP Aus.	1920s-77	HM	2	2-8	
NP Czech.	1925-77	HM	2	2-6	
NP W. Ger.	1950-77	MM	4	2-3	
NP E. Ger.	1952-77	HM	2	2-3	

Variant: Man in Cello 138, 139 L-S	1870s-1939	HM	1	18-20	Similar to clown in mandolin ornament.

C. LYRES

159B L-S	1870s-1939	F	1	10-15	Lyres may include glanzbilder in
159A W. Ger.	1960s	F	3	2-3	ornament design.

D. TUBAS

158A L-S	1870s-1939	F	2	8-10	
NP Aus.	1920s-77	F	2	2-8	Tubas actually produce sound
NP Czech.	1925-77	F	2	2-6	
NP W. Ger.	1950-77	F	3	2-3	
NP E. Ger.	1952-77	F	2	2-3	

E. ACCORDIANS
Symbol of Lauschan Glassblowers' Club, thus was gaffers' trademark.

NP L-S	1870s-1939	HM	2	15-18	
NP Aus.	1920s-77	HM	2	2-8	
NP Czech.	1925-77	HM	2	2-8	
159C W. Ger.	1950-77	MM	3	2-4	
NP E. Ger.	1952-77	HM	2	2-4	

F. TRUMPETS

158B L-S	1870s-1939	F	3	3-4	
NP Aus.	1920s-77	F	4	1-3	Trumpet ornaments play.
NP Czech.	1925-77	F	4	1-3	
NP W. Ger.	1950-77	F	4	1-2	
NP E. Ger.	1952-77	F	3-4	1-2	
NP Italy	1970s	F	4	2-3	

G. DRUMS

Used since pagan times to frighten away evil spirts during winter solstice.
Popular "Wild West" toy.

NP L-S	1880s-1939	HM	2	9-12	
NP Aus.	1920s-39	HM	3	7-9	
	1947-77	HM	2	2-3	Drumsticks missing on all
NP Czech.	1925-77	HM	2	2-8	ornaments.
155B W. Ger.	1950-77	MM	4	2-3	
NP E. Ger.	1952-77	HM	2	2-3	

H. HORNS

Also used in pagan times during winter solstice.

158C L-S	1870s-1939	F	3-4	3-4	
NP Aus.	1920s-77	F	3-4	1-3	
NP Czech.	1925-39	F	3-4	1-3	
NP W. Ger.	1950-77	F	4	1-2	
NP E. Ger.	1952-77	F	3	1-2	
NP Italy	1955-77	F	3	2-4	

I. MANDOLINS

155C, 157, 161A L-S	1870s-1939	F	1-2	15-20	Often elaborate with tinsel glanz-bilder, flowers, and crinkly wire
NP E. Ger.	1952-77	HM	2	2-4	trim. Shapes lend themselves to embellishment. Especially popular

Variant: Clown on mandolin.

156B L-S	1870s-1939	HM	1	18-20	around WWI.

J. SAXOPHONES

155A L-S	1870s-1939	HM	1	12-15

K. GUITARS

156C L-S	1870s-1939	HM	1	12-15
NP Czech.	1925-77	HM	1-2	2-8
NP W. Ger.	1950-77	MM	3-4	2-4

Nativity Symbols
Religious toys, figures, altars, and creches were in wide use around 1900, and Lauschans had extensive business of manufacturing them.

A. ANGELS

136A,C, 137, 140A, 141, 142A,C L-S	1870-1939	HM	1	20-35	Many different angel forms exist, depending on German region
NP W. Ger.	1950-77	MM	2-3	3-10	where made. Some have spun glass /paper wings, glass trumpet of
NP E. Ger.	1952-77	HM	2	3-10	Nürmberg angel, sold each year at Nürmberg Christmas Fair. Reputedly artist created a golden-haired angel doll to resemble his daughter who had died; this serves as model for most common angel ornament.
NP Italy	1955-77	F	3	5-6	Italian angels large, carry candy cane; other type has gold cardboard wings.

Variant: Angel with glanzbilder head

136B, 142B L-S	1905-10	HM	1	35

B. ANGEL HEADS

Putti heads common motif in German/Austrian churches.

140B L-S	1870-1939	HM	1	25-30	Scarcer than full-body form.
60B Aus.	1920s-39	HM	1	25-30	

C. CHRIST CHILD IN CRIB

NP L-S	1870-1939	HM	1+	75-100	In German museum.

D. CHRIST CHILD IN BALL	NP L-S	1870-1939	HM	1++	75-100	Glass ball has window opening: look inside to see Baby Jesus.
E. MADONNA AND CHILD	NP W. Ger.	1950-77	MM	2-3	2-4	Standing Madonna holding Infant in her arms.
F. STARS	163, 164B L-S	1870-1939	HM	1	10-15	Clear-cut star forms rarer than stars embossed on other forms.
	162 Czech.	1905-77	B	4	2-10	Usually small, but one star 2 feet in diameter has been reported.
	NP Aus.	1920s-39	HM	1	10-15	Czechs made 3 dimensional beaded stars for ornaments, tree tops.
	NP W. Ger.	1970s post-war II	MM	2-3	2-4	Relatively uncommon ornament considering prominence of star in
	160, 165A USA		MM	3-4	1-2	Nativity story.

Nautical Pieces

A. ANCHORS Popular Victorian motif, used with cross/heart for faith/hope/charity.	165-6 L-S	1870s-1939	F	1+	50-75	Often ornament made incorporating heart/cross. May be trimmed with scrap angel.
B. SAILBOATS Common motif on Valentines, postcards,etc.	143A,C, 144 L-S	1870s-1939	F	2	15-50	Passengers were glanzbilder; often boats were covered by crinkly wire. Many had cardboard sails, tinsel rigging. Some sailing ships measure up to 18" ($50-75). Newer "masts" often plastic.
	NP Czech.	1905-77	B	3-4	2-4	
	143B Czech.	1925-38	F	2	15-30	
	NP W. Ger.	1950-77	F	3-4	2-5	
	NP E. Ger.	1952-77	F	2	2-5	
C. STEAMBOATS 1860 marked the advent of the steamship.	NP L-S	1890-1939	HM	1+	60-80	Includes a few warships.
	NP W. Ger.	1950-77	HM	1-2	3-5	

Oddities

·Oddity ornaments were usually hand-blown as "whimsies" to satisfy a creative urge or help wile away the time of the glass-maker.

A. THREE-FACED ORNAMENTS Resembles a bisque fairy lamp of this period.	167-9 L-S	1870s-1939	HM	1	35-40	Faces include dog, cat, owl, all with exceptionally well-painted eyes to resemble Lauschan glass eyes.
B. TWO-FACED DOGS	172-4 L-S	1870s-1939	HM	1	10-15	Obverse and reverse have same dog face in relief. Small.
C. BIRD-THOR FACES	170-1 L-S	1870s-1939	HM	1	35-40	Clever ornament: bird hangs in usual fashion, self-hook on back. Turned backward, face of Thor is revealed on bird's abdomen, neck of bird becomes Thor's cap, and tail of bird is Thor's beard.
D. STRANGE ORNA-MENTS WITH EXTENDED ARMS	175 L-S	1900-30	F	1	20-25	Sometimes ornament's "arms" support bells or acorns or fruits. Moveable. See also "TREES".

Paradise Play Figures

See TEXT for discussion.

A. DEVILS	175A,B L-S	1870-1939	HM	1-2	20-25	Devil ornament available in both silvered, clear glass.

B. SNAKES

176C L-S		1870-1939	F	2	8-15	Usually colored on body curl only, some have multicolor stripes. Comes in large and small sizes.
NP W. Ger.		1950-77	F	2	2-5	
NP E. Ger.		1952-77	F	2	2-5	

C. APPLES

145 L-S		1870-1939	F	1-2	2-20	Usually have fabric or paper leaves on stem.

Patriotic Items

Uncle Sam, John Bull, symbols of America and Great Britain, Red, white, and blue America's national colors.

A. UNCLE SAM IN R/W/B STOCKING	148 L-S	1870-1920s	HM	1	25-35	Ornament made exclusively for import to USA.
B. R/W/B BELLS Could represent American liberty bell.	146 L-S	1870-1920s	HM	4	4-7	Ornament made exclusively for import to USA.
C. R/W/B STRIPED FORMS: balls, etc.	147 L-S	1870-1920s	F	4	3-5	Ornament made exclusively for import to USA.
D. JOHN BULL	NP L-S	1880-1914	HM	1	25-35	Ornament made exclusively for import to England and colonies.

People Ornaments

A. ELVES	149B L-S	1870s-1939	HM	2	10-15	Hard to distinguish from clowns/ character doll ornaments.
	NP Italy	1955-77	F	3	6-7	Representations of the "Seven Dwarfs."
	NP USA	1971-77	MM	3	3-4	One of figurals made by Harold Echardt, son of Max Echardt. Resemble Italian ornaments.
B. COMIC STRIP CHARACTERS						
1. Happy Hooligan A loveable pathetic personage.	193B L-S	1900-39	HM	1	50	Happy, from strip created by F.B. Opper in 1899, appeared in Hearst papers through 1936; featured sad face, empty tin can hat.
2. Foxy Grandpa An ageing, mischievous prankster.	193A L-S	1900s-39	HM	1	45-50	Strip originated by Charles E. Schultze, included famous people in episodes.
3. Betty Boop Essentially dumb, frivolous French-doll type.	NP L-S	1920-39	HM	1	50-65	Both movie and cartoon comic character produced by Max Fleischer: 1915-30s.
4. Andy Gump Known for appalling lack of lower jaw	NP L-S	1920-39	HM	1	50-60	Strip created by Robert S. Smith and Gus Edson: 1917-40s. Adventures with his wife, Min, son, Chester.
C. MOVIE STARS						
1. Mary Pickford a. Head b. Full figure "America's sweetheart" had famous blond tresses.	196A L-S 193C	1920-39 1920-39	HM HM	1 1	35 50-60	Both actress and producer, often played childrens' roles. Ornaments of 2 types: figural and head in relief on basic form.
2. Keystone Kops Perfect comedy foil as they were symbols of dignity and authority.	193D	1913-39	HM	1	50-60	Burlesque comedians, created by Max Sennett between 1912-17.
3. Al Jolson Popular singer/actor (1886-1950), known especially for minstrel shows.	196B L-S	1909-39	HM	1	60-75	Seen as "black man" ornament from his famous role as "Mammy" in 1909 show.

4. Charlie Chaplin Beloved comedian of Germany and US.	NP L-S	1912-20	HM	1	50-60	Ornament shows dancing figure, battered hat/cane.
D. BOOK CHARACTERS 1. Kate Greenaway Produced famous child: bustle in back, large, puffed hat.	NP L-S	1870s-1939	HM	1	50-60	Artist drew children's pictures, valentines, Christmas cards; orna- ment captures hat, characteristics of Greenaway figure.
E. MOVIE CARTOON CHARACTERS 1. Popeye First American"superman."	NP L-S	1930s-39	HM	1	50-60	Ornament features sailor hat, prominent jaw holding corn cob pipe. From strip/movie cartoons: 1929-77.
2. Snow White and the 7 Dwarfs	194 USA	1938	HM	1+	set 250	Ornaments had limited sales (under name of Doubl-Glo) due to lack of general appeal. 1st AMERICAN figurals.
	NP Italy	1955-77	F	3	6-7	See ELVES under PEOPLE.
3. Disney Characters a. Mickey Mouse	NP Italy	1955-77	F	3	8-10	Typical Italian figures utilizing
b. Donald Duck		1955-77	F	3	6-8	much trim on lightweight, silver-
c. Minnie Mouse		1955-77	F	3	6-8	lustre glass forms.
F. FOLK CHARACTERS 1. Women Witches	149A L-S	1870s-1939	HM	1	50-65	Represents witch in fairy tale, "Hansel and Gretel;" many fairy tale characters made.
	NP Italy	1955-77	F	4	6-7	Has wooden broomstick, synthetic hair.
2. Man Peasant (farmer)	NP L-S	1870s-1939	HM	1	10-12	
3. Black Baby	149C L-S	1870s-1939	HM	1	50-60	Child has tiny earrings molded in ears.
4. Boy	201B Czech.	1925-55	F	1	8-10	Simplistic forms have detailed painting (matte finish), glitter,
5. Soldier	201A Czech.	1925-55	F	2	8-10	silk and felt trim. Typical.
6. Boy Peasant	201C Pol.	1934-39	F	1+	20-25	One of VERY FEW Polish figurals made. Basic pin-ball shape; rather crude painting details, use glitter/ paint.
7. National Characters	177 Italy	1955-77	F	3	6-9	Extensive variety of figurals, dis- tinctive for handblown extremities, later annealed to body of ornament. Much trim: fur, plush, feathers,
8. Soldier	NP Italy	1955-77	F	3	3-5	paint, glitter, maribou, flocking. Lightweight, lustred glass.
9. Peasant Girl	197A Russia	1976	HM	2	5-10	Also make spacemen, dog, fish figurals; sold in GUM's Dept. Store, Moscow. Heavy glass,
10. Cossack Santa	197B Russia	1976	HM	1	5-10	unmarked cap, wide color range. Very little paint detail, lacquer wash over ornament. Distinctly Russian.
G. FAMOUS PERSONALITIES Staffordshire potters in England making figurines of famous people during this period: Disraeli	202 L-S	1870s-1939	HM	2	60-75	German glass-blowers filled requests for specific ornaments from England and other countries as well as the US. Prime Ministers popular subjects.

Royalty Items

Royal families were prevalent in 19th and 20th century Europe; the crown was symbolic of pre-eminence and leadership.

A. HANDBELLS WITH CROWN HANDLE

198B L-S	1870s-1939	HM	1	15-20	Very rich color on ornament, embellished with metallic gold.

B. SINGLE CROWNS

198C L-S	indefinite	HM	1	10-15	Crowns may have been made upon request of English buyers, as they were made on special order only; earliest known crown ornament made in 1885.

C. HEADS WEARING CROWN

198A L-S	1870s-1939	HM	2	12-15	

D. ROYALTY FIGURES
Staffordshire figures of Royal Families, prominent national leaders, popular in England; may have served as ornament models.

NP L-S	1880-1900	HM	1	125-150	Ornaments included representations of Prince Albert, Queen Victoria, etc.

Santa Claus/St. Nicholas

The personification of centuries of legend, Santa Claus is the amalgamation of Thor, Kriss Kringle, and Saint Nicholas. Santa Claus ornaments are second most common figurals made.

A. COMMON FORMS

179B, 180E, 182, 199C	L-S	1870-1939	HM	3	8-12	"Clausmen' usually torsos, Santas with long coats being more collectible. Many colors: red, green, silver, yellow, blue, gold, and white. Usually hang, but may have clip-ons. Czech. Santas carry bag of goodies or nothing; German carry tree. Contemporary Aus. Santas not more than 2½".
199A, 180A	Aus.	1920-39	HM	3	8-12	
199B	Czech.	1925-39	HM	3	8-12	
NP	Jap.	1921-41	MM	2-3	5-7	
NP	USA	1939-40	MM	1	25-30	Created by Corning, fullbodied.
NP	W. Ger.	1950-77	MM	4	2-4	Heavily painted, not too much detail.
NP	E. Ger.	1952-77	HM	3	2-4	Some miniatures as well.
NP	Italy	1955-77	F	3	5-7	Has real fur beard, tubular shape.

B. VARIANTS:

1. Full-bodied Santa	184 L-S	1870s-1939	HM	2-3	15-17	Has composition boots, chenille legs. Relatively few made.
2. Santa in Chimney	179A, 183A L-S	1870s-1939	HM	2	15-20	Comes in various sizes.
	NP W. Ger.	1970s	MM	4	3-5	Poor detail, various poses.
3. Santa on Pink Ball with Zodiac signs	179C L-S	1870s-1939	FHM	1	18-20	
4. Santa Head	178, 180B,D L-S	1870s-1939	HM	2	15-20	Scarcer than body types.
	NP Aus.	1970s	HM	3	2-4	Crudely painted.
5. St. Nick Riding a Horse	185 L-S	1880s-1920	HM	1	25-35	Horse's legs in bas-relief.
Horses, with free-standing legs, rare, except for Italian ornaments.	NP Italy	1955-77	F	3	6-8	Has separate Santa glued onto silvered horse, in saddle area.
6. Santa on Cone, in basket.						See CONES, See BASKETS.
7. Mrs. Santa Claus on cover.	L-S	1870s-1939	HM	1	18-20	Carries purse.
8. Santa with legs	181 L-S	1890-1920	HM	1	25	Arms missing on pictured Santa; stated value is for perfect Santa ornament.
9. Santa on ball	180C L-S	1870s-1939	HM	2-3	12-15	Plentiful use of wire/tinsel.
	183B Aus.	1920-39	HM	2	12-15	Painting suggest era.

Shells

Like the egg, the shell is regarded universally as one of the most beautiful forms in nature. Shells were widely used in Victorian times for making dolls, boxes, frames, banks, etc., known as "fairings" as they were commonly sold at village fairs.

A. CLOSED CLAM SHELL

					Remarks
187-8 L-S	1870s-1939	HM	1	5-8	Old as well as new shell ornaments may have clip as hangers. Closed clam shell popular; embossed shell rarer than plain ribbed shell. Available in various colors, some frosted. East Germany makes miniatures as well as standard sizes.
NP E. Ger.	1970-77	HM	2	2-3	

B. EMBOSSED SHELL

186 L-S	1870s-1939	HM	1	7-10

Snowmen

Building snowmen universally popular winter pastime of children. Bisque snowmen figurines appeared as "snow babies" with peak of manufacture at the turn of the century. Snowmen were also common form of German and Japanese candy containers during same period. Also see INFANCY ITEMS.

					Remarks
203A L-S	1880s-1939	HM	2	10-15	Earlier snowmen usually finished in matte paint over "sandy" base, occasionally trimmed with crinkly wire, spun glass. Carry stick, red scarf, hat. By the thirties, eyes were decals on the faces. Newer snowmen may have dull white finish; usually hold brown stick, have black, ragged hat, painted eyes.
203B Aus.	1920s-77	HM	2	2-10	
NP W. Ger.	1950-77	MM	3	2-5	

Spherical Forms/ Geometrical Shapes/Elongated Ornaments

Balls represent circles of eternal life, perfect and never-ending.

A. SCHECKENS
Symbolic of 3 balls in St. Nicholas legend and Paradise Tree fruit.

					Remarks
NP Lauscha	1820-?	F	1+	75-125	Heavy glass ball, showing alternating bands of color and silver; corked, not capped. Glass by-products too heavy for commercial use.

B. KUGELS
Similar to schnecken except evenly silvered.

					Remarks
80 Lauscha	1860-?	F	1	25-75	Evenly-silvered, heavy glass ball. Corked, not capped at first. Later ones have embossed caps/rings. Rare color amethyst. Seen also in red, green, light green, blue, amber. No pink/purple. Size range: 1–18". Largest US collection: Tasha Tudor, book illustrator, artist.

Variant:
Kugel with 2 caps.

205 Lauscha	1860-?	F	1+	50	Has cap on either side for hanging.

C. WITCHES' EYES
Have been reported in France/Belgium as well. Hung on candletrows or in windows/fireplace as decoration/protection.

					Remarks
NP Italy	1600s	F	1+	250+	Most plain glass, some swirled, up to 15" in diameter; heavier than kugels. Seem almost to be one heavy ball within another to give a sense of depth kugels lack.
NP Eng.	1759	F	1+	250+	
NP USA	1840-1900s	F	1	45-250	

Appendices

D. TYPICAL ROUND BALLS
(in chronological order by dates)

First balls, paper-thin, made by Schlotfeger.	190 L-S 214 218 224B	1860s-1939	F	4	1-20	Thin-walled, lightweight, silvered internally, dyed and lacquered, trimmed with paint, fine wire, starch "snow," glass beads, or acid etching. Indents made from balls. Size range: 1–15". Occasionally twisted for effect.
First American Ornaments	NP USA	1870s-?	F	U	****	First US glass-blowers making silvered bead/balls; unidentified craftsmen, largely. See TEXT.
Beaded Ornaments	216 Czech.	1905-77	B	4	2-4	Tiny silvered, colored balls (beads) strung on wires to form ornament shapes. May be 3-dimensional.
Czechoslovakian ornaments	NP Czech.	1925-77	F	4	1-6	Usual common balls/indents, some trimmed.
Japanese ornaments	NP Jap.	1920s-77	F+ MM	4	10c-$1	Early/later balls marked "Japan;" post-war balls labelled "Made in Occupied Japan" (1947-51). Cruder glass, heavyweight, harsh colors. Miniatures preferred after WWII.
Austrian ornaments	NP Aus.	1920s-77	F	4	1-5	Made by firm, "Wiener Christbaumschmuck Fabrik," Vienna; largest company. Also as a "cottage industry" centered around Vienna. Much trim/detail/hand painting.
Polish ornaments	221A Pol.	1930-77	F	4	25c-$3	Frequently trimmed with matte paint/glitter. Figurals fashioned from these basic shapes, very simple forms.
Polish Indents	189 Pol.	1930-77	F	3-4	25c-$4	Many indents have typical pear-shape with tip on bottom. Typical decoration. See TEXT.
American ornaments	NP USA	1934	F	4	?	Few assorted balls produced by Paper Novelty Co., (Doubl-Glo), insignificant.
1st complete American ornament production: Angelo Paione, Newark, N.J.	NP	1935	MM	U		Unique ornaments: special silver solution applied to ornament exterior, then lacquered for added brilliance/durability. No extant examples.
1st large-scale production of machine made ornaments	204A,B	1939-40	MM	2	25c-$4	By Corning Glass Works. Short pike, uniform, fairly thick glass, indents common. War-time balls: clear glass decorated with paint in various striped patterns, paper caps, no silvering. Blanks shipped to other firms for finishing.
"Shiny Brite"	204C	1939-40- 1977	MM	4	10c-$1	Max Echardt begins full-scale production under name "Shiny Brite," using Corning blanks. Other firms follow: George Francke, Baltimore, Maryland.
West German ornaments	215 W.Ger.	1950-77	MM	4	10c-$8	Balls in "old-world" style in addition to plain ones; older motifs, glitter, paint, crystallizations, frostings. Indents. Newer balls often clear glass with trim or decorations inside.
Colby Glass Company	NP USA	1952-77	MM	4	10c-$1	Colby Glass begins production, using Corning blanks.

East German ornaments	NP E. Ger.	1952-77	HM	2	1-7	"Old-world" ornaments in very limited supply, usually with poor workmanship due to age of artisans, but with exciting colors: brick red, silver-greens, grayed-blues. Some hand-painted.
Italian ornaments	NP Italy	1955-77	F			Typical Italian workmanship.
Collectors' Series 191, 213, 217	USA	1972-77	MM	3	3-7	Dated balls (usually), with applied silk-screen patterns. See CHART.
Krebs und Sohn, Roswell, New Mexico	192B	1974-77	MM	3-4	1-4	Balls usually pastel colors trimmed with braid, jewels, crystallizations, paint, fine wire, embroidery, and silk-panel inserts.
E. STRINGS OF BEADS	NP L-S	1870s-1939	F	2	1-12	Usually 4' long, composed of lustre-finish, round/egg shaped beads in assorted colors. Beads about 1" in diameter, some indented.
	NP USA	ca. 1854	HM	U		Blown by Wm. DeMuth. (see TEXT).
	NP Jap.	1920s-77	MM	3-4	1-3	Earlier strings included round and indented shapes. Later strings occasionally diamond-shaped. Many bead forms, but very late strings always composed of TINY elements.
	NP Czech.	1976-77	F	4	1-2	Large beads with tips on each bead; each string about 1 foot long.

Toys

Toy-makers and ornament-makers shared essentially the same area in Germany; many ornaments were almost exact copies of toys being made during the same period.

A. TEDDY BEARS Toy designer, Marguerite Steiff, created 1st Teddy Bear, based on Teddy Roosevelt cartoon, showing Roosevelt over dead bear he shot in the Rockies. Ornament modelled after the toy, a standard toy item in 1906.	244-5 L-S	1906-39	HM	2	30-35	"Teddy" bear always full-faced, showing abdomen, arms extended at sides, sitting or standing.
	NP W. Ger.	1950-77	MM	4	3-7	Newer "Teddy" featured in many poses. Wide range in workmanship.
	NP E. Ger.	1952-77	HM	2	3-7	
	NP Italy	1955-77	F	3	5-7	Italian "Teddy" usual form but brown body is covered with brown flocking.
	NP Jap.	1974	MM	1	15	"Cinnamon Bear," made on special order.
B. TOPS (Dreidls) Fancy tops made in countless varieties, illustrated in LA NATURE, French magazine, 1896.	228 L-S	1870s-1939	F	3	5-10	Most often large ornaments trimmed with paint or in fancy frosted patterns.
	NP Italy	1955-77	F	3	4	
C. DOLLS Models for doll ornaments probably character dolls made in Nürnberg and environs.	195, 243 L-S	1870s-1939	HM	1-2	15-20	
	NP Italy	1955-77	F	3	6-8	These ornaments include Raggedy Ann/Andy in usual tubular form, plaid dress and suit.
D. CORNUCOPIA OF TOYS	229 L-S	1870-1930s	HM	1	30-35	Various toys in bas-relief barely discernible: doll, bugle, book, etc.
E. STOCKING WITH TOYS	164					See: HOUSEHOLD ITEMS.

Transportation Items

Please also see NAUTICAL ORNAMENTS.

	Refs	Type	Country	Date		No.	Price	Notes
A. AIRSHIPS	206, 208-10,							
1. Captive Balloons Sport reached peak of popularity around 1900.	225-7	L-S		1870s-1939	F	2	18-25	Balloons often elaborately etched, rigged with tinsel, fine wire. Passengers were glanzbilder: Santas, angels, children.
		NP	W. Ger.	1950-77	F	3	2-5	
		NP	E. Ger.	1952-77	F	2	2-5	
2. Dirigibles	207, 212, 222	L-S		1870s-1939	F	1	35-50	Made in sardine/gondola forms, various colors. Most often see the 'Los Angeles' ornament copy of Zeppelin Works World War I reparation dirigible, made in Germany for US.
		NP	W.Ger.	1950-77	F	3	2-5	New German airships good copies of old, but heavier.
		NP	Italy	1955-77	F	3	7-9	New Italian airship is rocket with Santa aboard.
		NP	E. Ger.	1952-77	F	1		
3. Airplanes Wright Brothers made first flight in 1903; by World War I each major country had an airforce.	211	L-S		1920s	HM	1+	25-35	Few airplanes made possibly due to difficulty in manufacturing them and fragility.
	242	Czech.		1905-77	B	2	8-10	3-dimensional ornaments.
B. AUTOMOBILES First car produced in 1886; commercially available around 1900, plentiful by 1920.	223	L-S		1890s-1939	HM	2	15-50	Car ornaments vary in style, none distinctive enough to be definitive as to make/exact date of manufacture except Volkswagen "bug" of West Germany. Occasionally new car ornaments trimmed with glitter /paint.
			Tyrol region of Aus.	1933-34	HM	2	15-20	
	224	W. Ger.		1950-77	MM	2	2-4	
		NP	E. Ger.	1952-77	HM	2	2-4	
C. TRAINS		NP	L-S	1870s-1939	HM	1+	30-45	Usually single cars.
		NP	W. Ger.	1950-77	MM	3	5-7	New West German trains made from molds brought from Lauscha; even new ones not too plentiful.
D. TRAFFIC LIGHTS		NP	Lauscha only	1920-30	HM	1-2	12-15	
		NP	E. Ger.	1967-?	HM	1-2	3-6	Ornaments made in East Germany, but came in through West Germany.

Trees

Trees are symbols of eternal life, beloved since earliest pagan times. According to old legend, 3 trees- an olive, a date, and a pine–stood near the manger at Bethlehem. The olive gave the Christ Child a fruit, the second a date, but the pine had nothing, so the stars came down to rest on the pine's boughs; the Infant was so pleased He made the pine tree the first true Christmas tree. Another ancient story is about a poor, cold child taken in by a family on Christmas Eve. When the child departed the next morning, he went to a fir tree, broke off a branch, and stuck it into the ground, announcing it would be ever green and would bear fruit every Christmas in return for their goodness to Him.

Also see TEXT.

	Refs	Type	Country	Date		No.	Price	Notes
A. COMMON EVER-GREEN SHAPES	220B,C	L-S		1870s-1939	HM	2	5-7	Newer tree ornament in common shape almost exact copy of old.
		NP	W. Ger.	1950-77	MM	4	2-3	Painted dots resemble ornaments on a Christmas tree. Various sizes.
		NP	E. Ger.	1952-77	HM	2	50c-$3	Miniature trees made as well as standard sizes.

B. TREES WITH ORB BASE (large and small)	220A.	L-S	1870s-1939	HM	2	10-12	
C. TREES WITH FLATTENED SIDES	221 220D	L-S	1870s-1939	HM	1	12-14	Trees often use clip hanger as tree must rest on top of Christmas tree branch.
C. TREES SURROUNDED BY BELLS	219	L-S	1900-30	FHM	1	20-25	Also see "ODDITIES" for similar ornaments.
E. TREE SHAPES	NP	USA	1939-40	MM	1	9	One of rare Corning figurals. Rather heavy glass.
F. FLAT TREES	NP	Czech.	1905-77	B	4	2-3	Flat tree outline, usually made of little green beads.

Vases, hanging

Hanging vases are called by some collectors "hanging lamps," from their resemblence to oil/kerosene hanging lamps used commonly in the 19th century.

230-1, 246	L-S		1870s-1939	FHM	2	6-10	Vases often trimmed with artificial flowers, wire, paper leaves, beads, glanzbilder, feathers. chenille, tassels, maribou. Green fern-like material, "tucksheer" used as foliage, a kind of flocking. Various sizes.
	NP	Czech.	1905-77	B	2	2-4	
	NP	Czech.	1946-77	FHM	2	2-4	
	NP	W. Ger.	1950-77	FMM	3	2-4	
	NP	E. Ger.	1972-	FHM	2	2-4	
	NP	Italy	1955-77	F	3	3-4	

Vegetables

A. PICKLES Few pickle ornaments made as glass-blowers held cucumbers in low esteem.	247	L-S	1870s-1939	HM	1	25	Came in various shapes: dills, gherkins, etc.
B. PEAS-IN-A-POD	NP	L-S	1870s-1939	HM	1++	75	Described in old ornament catalogues.
C. EARS-OF-CORN	250B	L-S	1870s-1939	HM	1-2	25	Corn generally unpopular with Germans who considered it pig swill.
	NP	E. Ger.	1947-52	HM	3		
D. TOMATOES	79B, 248	L-S	1870s-1939	HM	1	25	Although commonly considered a vegetable, tomatoes are fruits.
E. CARROTS	250A	L-S	1870s-1939	F	2	20-22	Usually have "tucksheer" sprouting from ornament top.
F. MUSHROOMS	236, 238	L-S	1870s-1939	F	3	2-4	Appears as single or double form; usually clip on.
	235	Aus.	1920s-77	F	3	2-3	Smaller than Lauschan ones.
	NP	Jap.	1920s-41	MM	3	1-2	
	NP	W. Ger.	1950-77	F	4	1-2	
Variant: Santas Under Mushroom Hat	233	L-S	1870s-1939	HM	2	8-10	German/Japanese Santa ornament essentially same, but are of different quality; Japanese mushroom "hat" is so thin it resembles a lid. Clip-on hanger.
	NP	Jap.	1920s-1941	MM	2	6-8	
G. PUMPKINS/SQUASH	249	L-S	1870s-1920	HM	1	8-10	Small.
Variant: Jack O'Lantern	237	L-S	1880-1920s	HM	1	15-18	
	NP	Jap.	1925-39	MM	1	8-10	

H. FANTASY ROOT VEGETABLES	234 L-S	ca. 1930	F	2+	6-8	Deep purple color.

Victorian Swings

"Swinging" was frequent recreation of coy Victorian ladies, reflected not only in glass Christmas ornaments but in toy swings which were driven by toy steam engines. These toy swings were made of wood, composition, or bisque and featured cotton batting figures.

NP L-S	1880s-1910	HM	1+	100-125	Ropes of tinsel held a clear glass seat, occupant either a glass boy or girl. Often decorated with artificial flowers/leaves.

Windmills

Windmills were widely used in the United States beginning about 1900, as an aid in both agricultural and food processing. Windmill design competitions were held throughout the country, and many outlandish structures resulted. Windmills served as a popular model for both toymakers and ornament-makers.

A. REGULAR FORMS

241A,B L-S	1890s-1939	HM	2	10-12	Glanzbilder often used as "arms"
241C Czech.	1905-39	B	3	3-6	of windmill. Occasionally see
	1946-77	B	2	2-4	windmills in bas-relief on various ornament shapes; some bead forms.
239 E. Ger.	1952-77	HM	2	2-15	Some very large; some iridescent, highly colored.

B. VARIANT

240 L-S	1890s-1939	F	1-2	25	An elaboration of simple form transforms it into windmill with tinsel arms.

Walnuts

Walnut glass ornaments were copies of nuts gilded as Christmas decorations used in the early 19th century.

See also ACORNS.

232 L-S	1870s-1939	HM	3-4	1-2	Ornaments appear in both silver
NP Aus.	1920s-77	HM	3-4	1-2	and gold.
NP Czech.	1925-77	HM	3-4	1-2	
NP W. Ger.	1950-77	MM	4	1	Small nut ornaments usually marked West Germany even
NP E. Ger.	1952-77	HM		1	though they are East German.

Index to Ornament Categories

APPENDIX 6

Map of Important Ornament Producing Regions

APPENDIX 7

Customs Information From 1921 Through 1975

Quantities of ornaments (by dollar values) imported into the United States by country, when available in records (records by individual country unavailable until 1934).

Years

1921	Duty	No record	
1922	35%	156,903	Principally German, Czech. bead ornaments,
1923	55%	251,415	few Austrian and Japanese ornaments
1924		359,349	
1925		452,731	
1926		602,008	
1927		926,010	
1928		993,143	
1929		886,043	
1930	60%	200,334	Passage of Hawley-Smoot Act
1931		569,262	
1932		552,486	
1933		416,664	

Years	Austria Duty		Germany Duty		Czechoslovakia Duty	
1934	112	60%	448,654	60%	8,214	60%
1935	2,092		911,648		42,023	
1936	456		854,118		48,522	
1937	7,033		1,015,436		147,776	
1938			833,000		74,000	
1939			633,000		7,000	
1940			7,308			
1941						
1942						
1943						
1944						
1945						
1946					17,000	50%
1947			W. Germany		40,351	60%
1948		50%	7,284	50%	64,990	
1949	205		71,907		30,003	
1950	44		596,744		89,002	
1951	539		958,155[2]		49,022	
1952	1,233		326,428		1,805	
1953	4,662		508,392		273	
1954	26,204		553,012			
1955	23,128		596,730		4,757	
1956	56,351		721,220		8,179	
1957	48,110		785,314		8,126	
1958[3]	64,046	25.5% / 40%	666,837	25.5% / 40%	38,319	60%
1959	91,708		711,269		91,602	
1960	93,404		850,000		92,417	
1961	85,144		1,070,525		138,618	
1962	158,094		1,040,254		118,519	
1963	27,985		620,267		23,284	
1964	223,581		1,166,224		60,531	
1965	207,298		1,197,614		82,535	
1966	112,782		1,465,476		98,460	
1967[3]	210,566	12.5% / 20%	1,564,148	12.5% / 20%	130,767	60%
1968	129,302		1,297,004		139,887	
1969	144,191		1,676,079		248,506	
1970	85,114		2,039,311		129,459	
1971	105,459		1,696,326		81,072	
1972	159,183		1,687,711		94,217	
1973	263,015		2,692,358		144,452	
1974	237,000		1,132,000		unlisted	
1975	137,000		779,000		99,000	

Totals since 1934

Germany and East Germany = $33,724,497
Japan =   17,492,472
Poland =   14,598,868

[1] Includes Germany & Austria – Years 1938 & 1939
[2] Includes East & West Germany
[3] Split duties depending upon price of ornaments inaugurated in 1958.
  Lessor duty assessed on higher priced ornaments – over $7.50/gross.

Poland	Duty	Japan	Duty	East Germany	Duty	Italy	Duty
3,896		9,365	60%				
32,998		27,833					
52,755		35,357					
31,709		73,955					
72,000		38,000					
96,000		48,000					
		116,964					
		45,081					
		1,000					
56	60%	1,200				380	
61,133		261,805	50%			976	50%
260,573		563,850				29	
247,061		801,323				851	
245,541		888,847				1,553	
443,608		439,813		549,335		24	
366,939		330,118		22,426	60%	2,964	
429,200		401,347		69,021		6,454	
452,718		449,955		25,147		22,072	
683,881		555,316		16,504		42,231	
482,510		600,261		18,495		122,355	
504,597	60%	441,696	25.5% / 40%	17,755	60%	164,480	25.5% / 40%
625,661		528,710		12,492		89,411	
631,739		529,538		12,508		89,482	
833,424		55,651				75,868	
916,575		900,582				62,236	
140,507		422,104				54,129	
576,580		832,491		894		48,100	
567,191		819,624				69,438	
647,968		918,658				176,376	
608,222	60%	1,182,973	12.5% / 20%	3,721	60%	168,037	12.5% / 20%
649,312		1,060,355		5,340		121,715	
607,403		1,020,871		2,858		138,460	
581,799	12.5%	695,306		5,000		131,746	
820,374	20%	560,191		30,065		177,427	
639,488		568,658		62,337		295,212	
596,450		648,046		68,885		326,364	
493,000		678,000		unlisted		334,000	
557,000		152,000		unlisted		421,000	

All information given
here pertains to the specific
ornament which is
illustrated.

1. Alligator, ca. 1910, large,
9" long.
2. Hedgehog, ca. 1900; photo
courtesy Joe Lindquist, Omaha.
3. Rabbit eating carrot (L)
ca. 1880; squirrel (R), ca.
1900.
4. Late pig, 1930's.
5. Old bear has legs in natural
position, unlike Teddy Bears;
Photo courtesy J. Lindquist,
Omaha.
6. Early basket, ca. 1900 (A);
more ordinary basket (B),
ca. 1920.

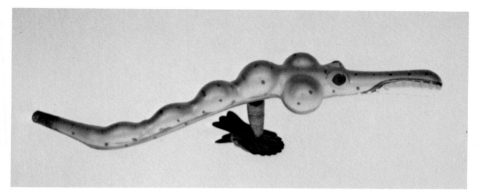

1

2

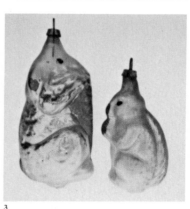

3

5

4

6

63

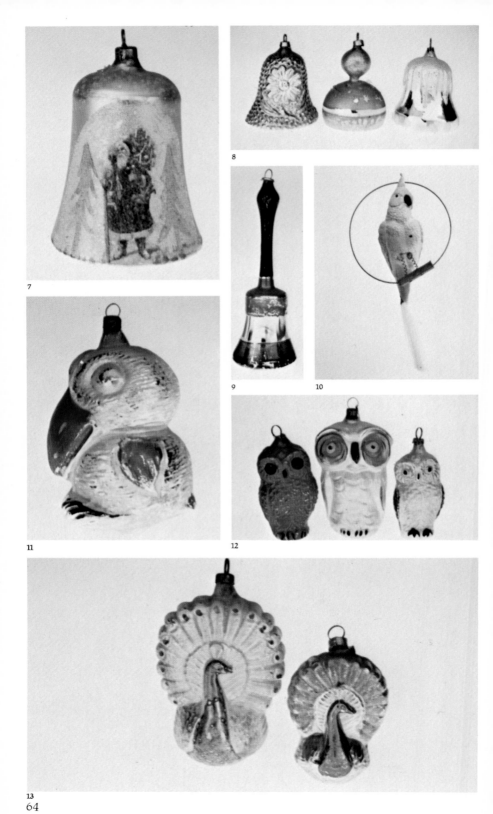

7

8

9

10

11

12

13

7. Bell has glanzbilder figure frosted with glass beads; early, ca. 1890.

8. Bells, (A) beaded, ca. 1900; (B) painted, (C) frosted, ca. 1920.

9. Relatively late handbell, fairly heavy glass, ca. 1925.

10. Unsilvered parrot, fantastic shading; early, ca. 1900.

11. Fat pelican carefully detailed, ca. 1900.

12. Note fine molding on "older" owls : A,C); (B) possibly '30's.

13. Exquisitely beautiful, fragile peacocks, very early, 1890.

14. Acorns (A,B) early; (C) is later, Austrian, ca. 1920.

15. Dog (B) earlier than dog (A) ca. 1920.

16. Both early Lauschan cats, ca. 1890-1900.

14

15

16

65

17

17. Very old bug; "sandy" wings; ca. 1910.
18. Rabbit-in-Egg "large" fantasy piece, ca. 1900.
19. Unsilvered penguin, '30's, German.
20. "New" frog (C), almost duplicates old (A); (B) old, also.
21. Two dogs (B,C) older than (A) dog; all whimsical.
22. Ornament-with-horse, probably early '20's.
23. Similar to 2-sided dog face; cf. plates 204-6; early.
24. Spider-in-web, probably turn-of-century.
25. All elephants very old, superb, ca. 1900.

18

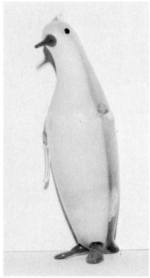

19

20

21

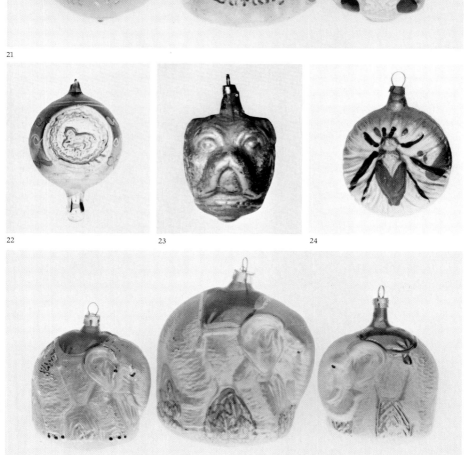

22　　　　　　　23　　　　　　　24

25

26. Dog-in-doghouse, very early; comes in several colors, ca. 1900.

27. German duck, probably '20's-'30's.

28. Both very old, fragile: monkey (A) ca. 1900, dog (B), ca. 1900.

29. Scotty dog, in unusual position, turn-of-century.

30. Small, unsilvered horse, '30's.

31. Complicated German octopus, '50's, blue.

32. Old German bear with muff; prime, early.

26

27

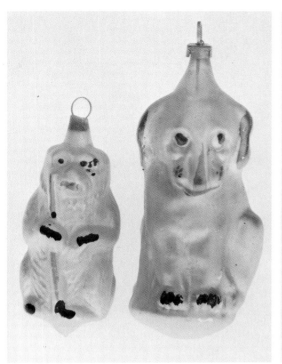

28

29

30

31

32

33. German dinosaur '50's, resembles Italian ornaments.
34. Very old pig, nose has been repaired; turn-of-century.
35. Very old Lauschan basket, scrap angel, ca. 1900.
36. Two baskets, probably '20's-'30's.
37. Santa-in-basket, likely near turn-of-century.
38. Blue/red unsilvered stork, ca. 1930; broken leg.
39. Song birds, dates undetermined.
40. Czech. wire-encased bird (A) and large Czech. bird (B), ca. 1930.

33

34

35

36

37

38

39

40

71

41. Unsilvered, blue-winged crane, '30's.
42. Awkward Japanese bird, tubular bill, '20's-'30's.
43. Blue Shiny-Brite bell, post-war.
44. All very early bells, ca. 1890-1910.
45. Handbell, probably '30's-'40's.
46. Newer German bell lacks separate clapper.

41

42

43

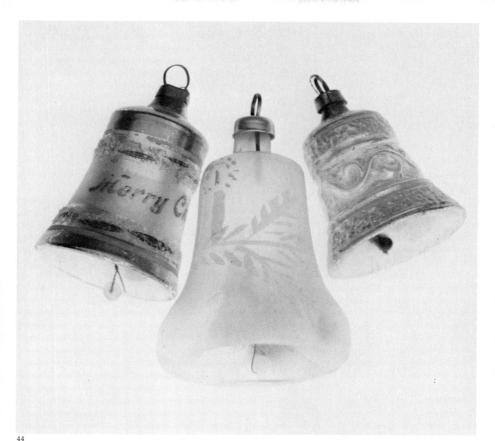

44

45   46

73

47. Magnificent early Lauschan bell with scrap figure, ca. 1890.
48-49. Two Czech. beaded bells, undetermined age, likely pre-war.
50. All old Lauschan birdhouses showing crow, raven, rooster.
51. Clown in middle "newer" than others.
52. New Italian harlequin, ca. 1958.

47

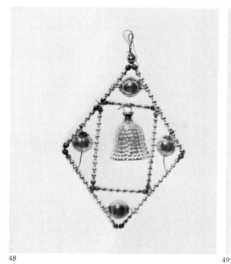

48

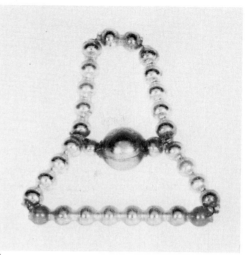

49

50

51

52

53

53. Girl jester, turn-of-century; photo courtesy J. Lindquist Omaha.
54. "New" heavy-glass clown (C), 2 older clowns on left (A,B).
55. Czech. cockatoo (B) noticeably less delicate than early German parrots.
56-57. Both birds/nests early; #57 more desirable.
58. Huge Czech. bird, moveable wings; ca. 1930's.
59. Paired storks/humming-birds, charming; 1920s; early fat turkey, ca. 1910.
60. Owls with glass tails, possibly the '20's.
61. Swan (C) very old; peacock with crown (A), flamingo (B) much later.
62. Beautiful but common song birds, early.

54

55

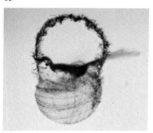

56

57

58

59

60

61

62

63. Early German stork; photo courtesy J. Lindquist, Omaha.

64. 1910 butterflies; moveable wings. Lovely.

65. Interesting butterfly shapes; fairly early.

66. Glass eyes on Ringmaster replaced by pearls, ca. 1900.

67. Unique early clown, indented body, ca. 1910.

68. Clown (A) earlier than clown (B).

69. Early clowns, middle one in stocking.

70. Fir cone with ribbon/ tucksheer, ca. 1920.

71. Japanese Santa on cone has Oriental expression, probably '20's.

72. Commonest doll head is (A); (B) head, early, unusual.

73. Classic "Baby Jesus" head in middle; boy's face on right.

63

64

65

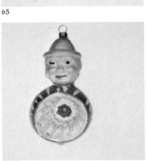

66

67

68

70

69

71

72

73

74

75

76

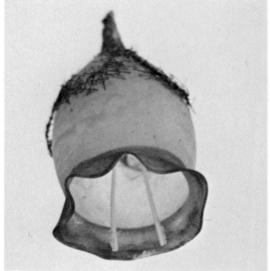

77

78

79

80

80

74. Very fine, early blowfish (A); early Lauschan gold-fish (B,C).

75. Beautiful early German rose (A), later Austrian rose (C), '20's tulip (B).

76. Turn-of-century trumpet flower (A) lotus pod (B) fragile, beautiful.

77. Calla lily, ca. 1910, large, handsome.

78. Strawberry/watermelon/grapes well-molded, probably ca. 1920's.

79. Exceptional coloring on pear/tomato/peach/ early, pre-1920.

80. Early kugel-like grapes, note ring hanger/ ca. 1880's.

81. Carousel (A) old, (B) is ca. 1930, and (C) is old.

82. Old clown heads rare, fine; modern head (A) relatively crude.

83. Early German, white pine-cone, ca. 1900.

81

82

83

84. Santa-on-cone (A) ca. 1925; common cone (B) of unknown age.
85. Missing eye on doll face (B) lessens value insignificantly.
86. Doll-head (B) newer than others; painted eyes less desirable than glass.
87. Jap. fish (middle), probably '30's; European fish older, 1910-20.
88. Daisy and "pedulas" probably '20's-'30's.
89. Lustrous yellow banana, early, ca. 1910.
90. Berries (A) and strawberry (C) after 1930; grapes early (frosted).

84

85

86

87

88

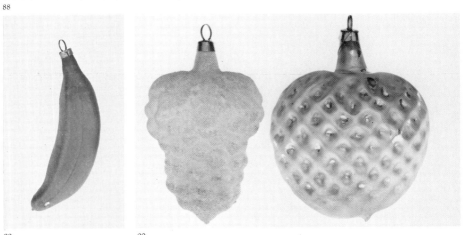

89   90

91. Yellow stippled lemon (A) and orange kumquat (B) unsilvered, old.
92. Orange unsilvered, old.
93. Plum, silvered, probably '30's.
94. Pear with candle-cup top, delicate and unsilvered; turn-of-century.
95. Unsilvered strawberries (B,C) very old; others probably '20's.
96. Berries (A) and grapes (B,C) probably '30's.
97. Both berries and heavy strawberry on right, '30's.
98. Fragile gun probably early 20th century.

91

92

93

94

95

96

97

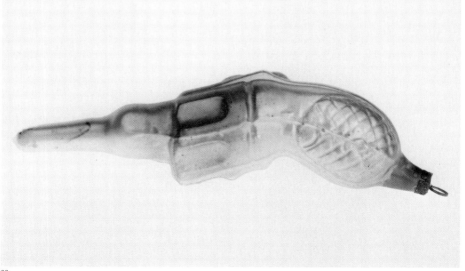

98

99

100

101

99-100. Austrian heart, 1930's, (#99) later than German hearts, ca. 1910 (#100).

101. "New" W. German heart (B); old German ones (A,C), ca. 1900.

102. All pipes of undetermined age; classic Bent Dublin on top.

103. Very old, frail umbrellas, ca. 1890.

104. Lady's shoes (A,C), man's shoe (B), styles reflect age; very early.

102

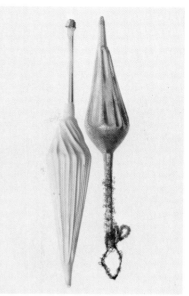

103

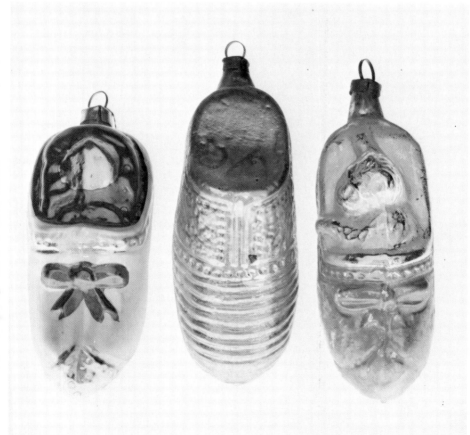

104

105. Old Christmas stocking, ca. 1890, shows doll, teddy bear, etc.
106. USA post-war lantern (A); '20's-'30's German lantern (B).
107. New German wine cask (B); old Lauschan ones (A,C), ca. 1910.
108. 'Malaga' bottle; bottles became popular during '20's, early '30's. (Prohibition era).
109. Sugar bowl (B) newer than coffee pots (A,C).
110. Old clock with paper face, ca. 1910; clock (A) 1930, clock (C) 1950's.

105

106

107

109

108

110

111. Red die, late 20's.
112. Czech. beaded stocking probably pre-WWII.
113. Red/green, large saddle shoe, 1950's.
114. Umbrella : A; turn-of-century; umbrella (B) 1920's-'30's.
115. Pink lantern (A) 1930's, lantern (C) probably 1920. Middle lantern, American, 1950's.
116. Cottage could be from 1920's.
117. Czech. beaded house (flat); between 1905-39.
118. First house (A) Austrian; likely '20's; church, other 2 houses, German 1910's-30's.
119. House, (B) '20's-'30's; (A) and (C) old, ca. 1900's, and (D) ca. 1910.

111

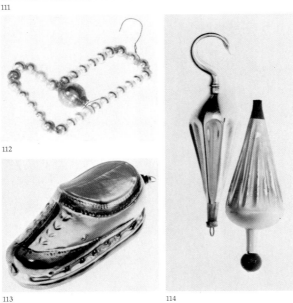

112

113   114

115

90

116

117

118

119

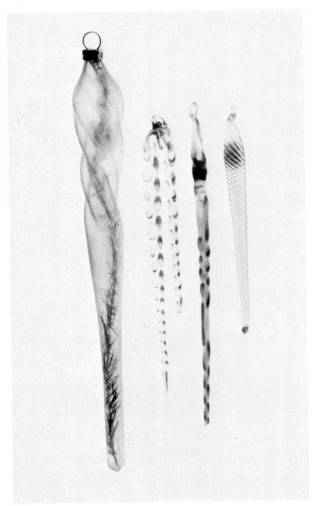

120. Icicles (B, D) very old; icicles (A, C) of undetermined age.
121. Icicles, '20's and '30's.
122. Pink pacifier, ca. 1910.
123. Flagon/ball of yarn, "fantasy pieces," ca. 1900; candle ca. 1920.
124. Fancy umbrella early German, ca. 1900.
125. Very large hunting horn; approx. 10", ca. 1880.
127. Coin-purse in style of period.
126. One of Three Little Pigs, German, 1930's.
128. Very early fox (B); later stag (A), prob. ca. 1920's.

120

121

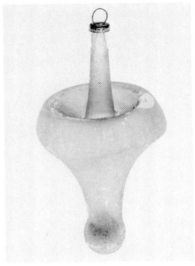

122

123

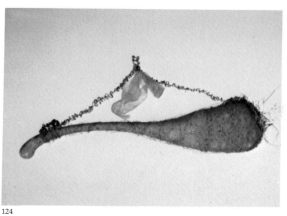

124

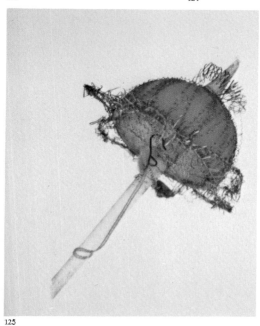

125

126

127

128

129

129. All early Indian ornaments; fantastic workmanship,
ca. 1890.
130. Early German-made
Indians (A,B); (C) is newer,
ca. 1920.
131-2. Boy on sled (front/
rear) "fantasy piece," ca. 1900.
133. Baby in tub viewed from
above; "fantasy piece," ca.
1900.
134. Early doll-head rattle,
ca. 1890.
135. Moon (A) much earlier
than moon (B), 1920's.
136. Rare "scrap angel" in
middle; photo courtesy Mott
Family.
137. Early Lauschan angels.
138-9. Front and rear views
of scarce Man-in-Cello, ca.
1910. (Mott Family).
140. Both relatively late angels.
141. Angel (A), classic type
with gold paper wings, angel
(B) blowing glass horn; early.
142. Angel head (B) early,
choice; angels (A,C) also early.

130

131

132

133

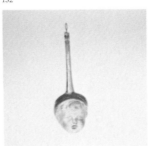

134

135

136

137

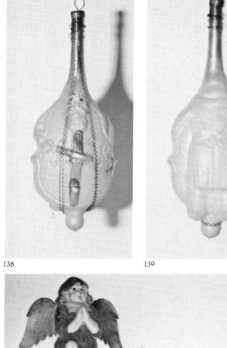

138

139

140

141

142

143

147

144

148

145

146

149

143. Boat (B) heavy, relatively late, 1930's; others earlier; ca. 1910.

144. Santa happy passenger in early gondola, ca. 1900.

145. Early (unsilvered) apple has fabric leaf, ca. 1910.

146-47. Wide variety of patriotic items, undated, perhaps WWI era.

148. Toe of Uncle Sam stocking broken/mended; "fantasy piece," ca. 1910.

149. All early characters; choice.

150. Czech. silver-beaded pacifier (A), ca. 1910; child (B), ca. late 1890's.

151. Baby rattle, ca. 1890's.

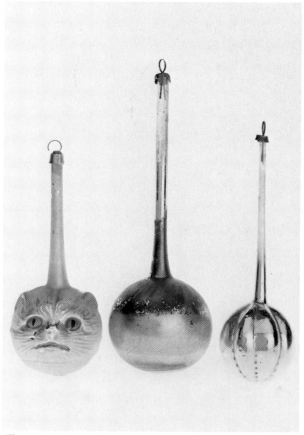

150

151

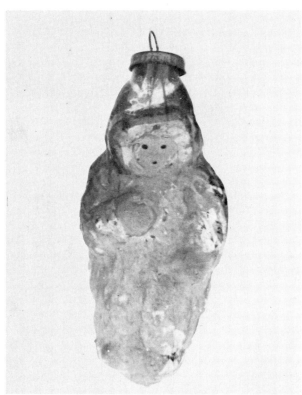

152. Snow-baby, very fragile, ca. 1910.
153. Table lamp (A) post-WWII; (B) old German, (turn-of-century), and (C) German, probably '30's.
154. Old standing lamp, ca. 1910.
155. White/purple saxophone (A), '20's-'30's; drum, (B) ca. 1965, tiny mandolin (C) '30's.
156. Cello (A) possibly 1930's, clown-on-mandolin (B), ca. 1910, and blue German guitar (C), ca. 1910.

152

153

154

155

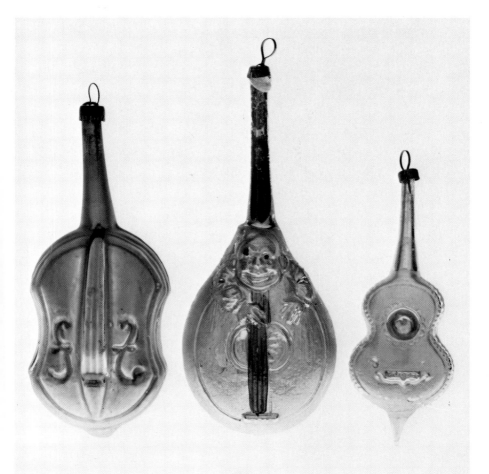

156

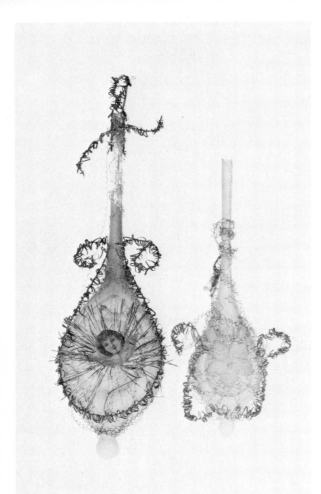

157. Exquisite Lauschan man-
dolins, ca. 1890.
158. Tuba (A) ca. 1930,
trumpet (B) ca. 1930, and horn
(C) earlier, ca. 1910.
159. Silver/gold lyre on ornament (A) 1960's, red lyre (B)
old German with glanzbilder,
ca. 1910, and accordian (C),
1950's.
160. Star-studded form,
probably American post-war.
161. Mandolin (A) possibly
'30's, violin (B) turn-of-century
162. Czech-beaded star,
undetermined age.
163. Both stars German: (A) is
ca. 1930, (B) is early, ca. 1900.

157

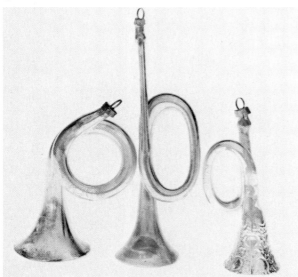

158

159

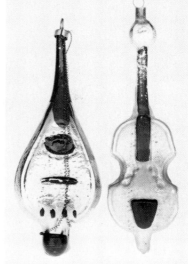

161

160

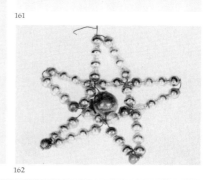

162

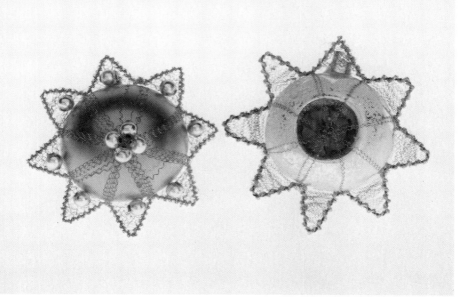

163

164

164. Star-indented ball (A) probably post-war American, (B) is German, ca. 1920.
165-66. Anchors with glanzbilder, ca. 1890; choice.
167-69. Odd 3-faced ornament (dog, owl, cat), probably ca. 1900.
170-71. Bird – Thor face ornament, probably turn-of-century; prime.
172-74. Two-faced dog, ca. 1925; 3 views; side, front, rear.

165

166

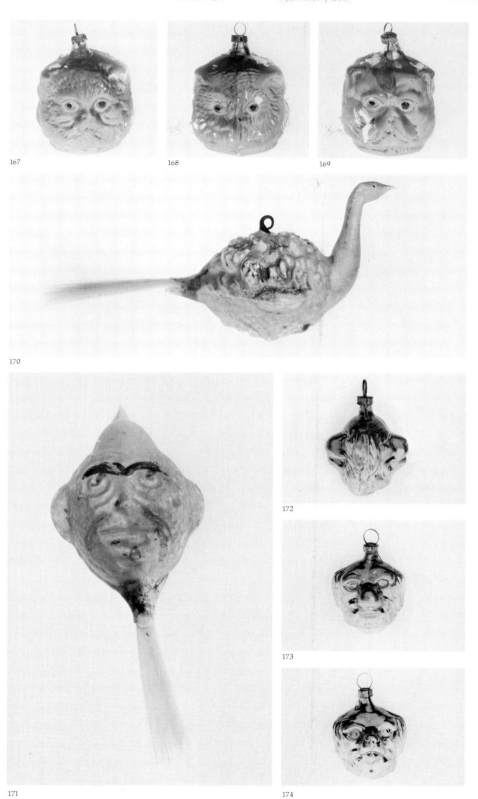

167

168

169

170

171

172

173

174

103

175

175. Both ornaments probably ca. 1930; moveable acorns.
176. Devils in Paradise Play: (A) is newer, ca. 1930, (B) ca. 1910. Silver snake is old, ca. 1910.
177. Italian national characters: Swiss, South American, US astronaut all 1950's.
178. All Santa heads, old Lauschan, pre-1925.
179. Charming Santa-in-chimney (A) ca. 1910; Lauschan Santa figure (B) same period, and (C) Santa-on-pink zodiac ball, ca. 1890.
180. Santa-with-toys (A) ca. 1925; miniature head (B) ca. 1900; Santa on big ball (C) ca. 1900; miniature head (D) ca. 1900; and unsilvered, sandy-finish Santa (E) ca. 1890.
181. Santa with free-form legs (arms missing), German, 1920's (Resemble comic strip/movie characters of same era.)
182. Traditional German Santa, (lacks clip), ca. 1920.
183. Small Santa in basket, (A,C) ca. 1900 and Santa-on-painted ball(B) ca. 1930.

176

177

178

179

180

181

182

183

184. Scarce Santa, ca. 1900;
chenille legs/composition boots.
185. "Fantasy piece" Santa-on-
horse, ca. 1890.
186. Enchanting pale-pink
shell, probably ca. 1900.
187. Closed clam shell (shell
clip), fairly old, ca. 1920.
188. Dark blue clam shell,
possibly late '30's, early '40's.
189. Lustrous indents: (A) is
Polish, ca. 1935, (B) is German,
with candle holder, ca. 1910.

184

185

186

187

188

189

190. Early Lauschan ball, wired, ca. 1890.
191. Collector's Series: Hallmark's Currier and Ives scene (small). See #217.
192. Krebs und Sohn (A) bell and (B) ball, 1974-77.
193. Foxy Grandpa, Happy Hooligan, Mary Pickford, Keystone Kop of same period; photo courtesy J. Lindquist, Omaha.
194. Snow White/7 Dwarfs; late '30's. (Mott Family).
195. Little German boy, character doll, early ca. 1910.
196. Pickford/Jolson heads, probably early '30's.
197. Contemporary Russian figures.

190

191

192

193

194

195

196

197

109

198. Head (A) later than crown items (B,C), ca. 1890.
199. "Mean" Father Christmas figure (A); common Santa (B); German Santa (C); all old.
200. Kate Greenaway, ca. 1920; photo courtesy J. Lindquist, Omaha.
201. Simplistic Czech (A) and Polish figures (B,C), '30's-'40's.
202. Disraeli; early, ca 1900.
203. Cap replaced on snowman (B), probably '20's.
204. Corning war-time ornament (A,B); post-war Shiny-Brite (C).
205. Early kugels; double hangers, on top; single hanger, below, ca. 1860-70.
206. Elegantly-wired balloons; early.
207. 'Los Angeles' zeppelin, '20's-'30's.

198

199

200

201

202

203

204

205

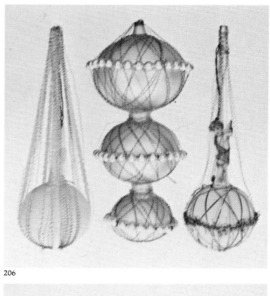

206

207

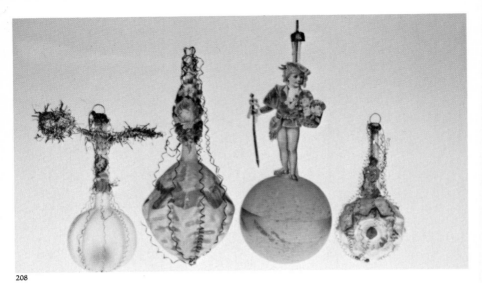

208

209

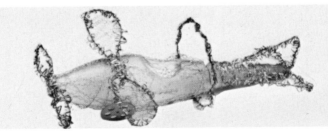

210

211

212

112

208-10. All early, choice balloons.
211. Rare airplane '20s; photo courtesy P. Snyder, N.Y.
212. Two gondolas, fairly early.
213. Collector's Series: (A) Hummel figure (1975-Schmid); (B) Walt Disney characters (1976-Schmid).
214. Indents: (A) German, ca. 1895; (C) German, ca. 1900; (B) German ca. 1930.
215. "Old-world" style, German post-WWII balls.

213

214

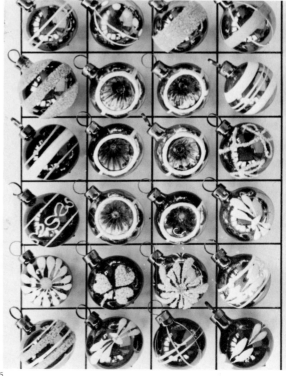

215

216. Czech beaded "fantasy"
(1905-77), exact date unknown.
217. 4 Collector's Series balls,
all by Corning Glass: (A)
Holly Hobby, (B) Nast's Santa
Claus (Drum Collection) (C)
Currier and Ives and (D) Bird
Edition.
218. Early fancy German
shapes, ca. 1920.
219. Odd German tree, bells
move, ca. 1930.
220. Trees: (A) with small orb
base; (B) common; (C) with
clip base; and (D) with
flattened sides. All fairly early
except (D).

216

217

218

114

219

220

221. Tree with large orb base, as above.
222. Indented gondola, wired, ca. 1910.
223. VW car: ca. 1955.
224. Old cars: top two, the 20's; bottom '30's vintage.
225. Very early fanciful balloon with tinsel, ca. 1890.

221

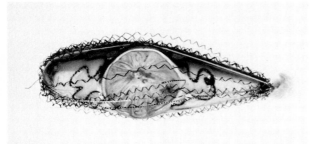

222

223

224

225

117

226. Two elongated balloons,
ca. 1900.
227. Single pale-pink, acid-
etched balloon: '20's-'30's.
229. Cornucopia of Christmas
toys, early, ca. 1900.

226

227

228

229

230. Fancy German hanging vase, ca. 1890-1900.
231. Spectacular vase, incorporating fabric flower, wire, ca. 1890.
232. Silver walnut, unknown age.
233. Santa under mushroom hat, delicately painted, turn-of-century.
234. "Fantasy" vegetable (purple carrot), probably ca. 1930.
235. Austrian mushroom, possibly late '30's.

230

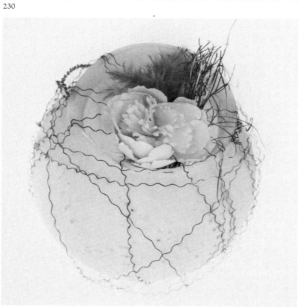

231

232

233

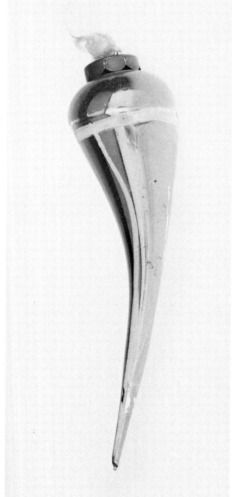

234

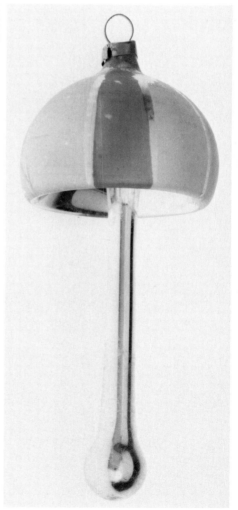

235

236. Big mushroom with heavy base, probably '30's.
237. Jack O'Lantern (German), early "fantasy piece", ca. 1910.
238. Standard mushrooms (A) single, (B) double, 1930's.
239. Turquoise E. German windmill, ca. 1952.

236

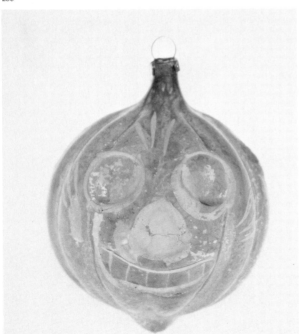

237

238

239

240. Windmill-airship, beautiful: ca. 1910.
241. Choice windmills: (A) with paper "arms", ca. 1910; (B) German, ca. 1900; and (C) Czech beaded, ca. 1950.
242. Beaded Czech. plane; '20's. (Snyder).
243. Early character doll; courtesy J. Lindquist, Omaha.
244-5. Characteristic Teddy Bears, ca. 1910.

246. Very early vases, all using "tucksheer."
247. Dill pickle, early; (Mott Family).
248. Unsilvered tomato.
249. Silvered pumpkin, fairly early, ca. '30's.
250. Corn (B) is much older than carrot (A).

240

241

242

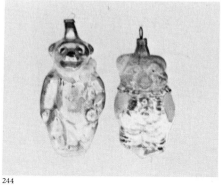
244

243

245

125

246

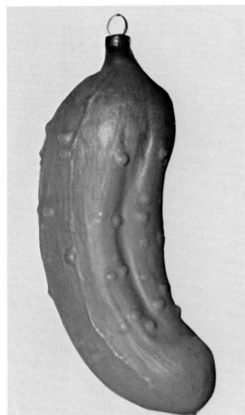

247

248

249

250